GAINING CO

THROUGH

THE MIND OF CHRIST

By

Beth Marie Rexford

Cover design by Ana Maria Mata

The author, unless otherwise noted, wrote all poetry.

All scriptures cited in the text, unless otherwise noted, are taken from the King James Version of the Bible. All Hebrew and Greek translations of words in scripture, unless otherwise noted, are taken from Strong's Exhaustive Concordance.

20% of all proceeds will be given to Foreign Missions towards the effort to send the glorious gospel of Jesus Christ to all nations.

Library of Congress Control Number: 2005907881

International Standard Book Number: 0-9771212-0-8

For additional copies of this book write to:

Triumphant Through Truth Publications
25083 Schafer Road
Clare IL 60111

Include $12.00 for each copy (add $2.00 per book for postage and handling)

Printed in the United States by Morris Publishing
3212 East Highway 30
Kearney, NE 68847
1-800-650-7888

Table of Contents

FOREWORD

From a life of depression, abuse, and chemical dependency, Beth Rexford exemplifies God's work of grace and supernatural deliverance. This book is not only Beth's expression of gratitude to God for the abundant life that He has given her, but it is the result of a journey still in progress. A journey that she began in an effort not only to know the Lord in an ever growing intimacy, but also to understand the dynamics that brought her to such despair and depression before His divine intervention.

In this book she opens her life to the reader and then carefully inter-weaves the principles of God's Word along with collected research data. The result is her first treatise addressing the *why's* and *how's* that dramatically began her personal transformation.

Beth has addressed subjects that very few dare to examine and she has done so with great passion and burden. Without a doubt this book will touch your heart and help renew your mind. I especially recommend it to those whose mind overwhelmingly battles between faith and secular reason. I have been Beth's Pastor since the day I baptized her and God filled her with the Holy Ghost. I stand amazed and rejoice at what the Lord is already doing through Sister Beth's life and this book.

Pastor Ric S. Gonzalez
International Christian Fellowship
Chicago

Isaiah 61:1-3

The spirit of the Lord God is upon me; because the Lord hath anointed me to preach good tidings to the meek; he hath sent me to bind up the broken-hearted, to proclaim liberty to the captives, and the opening of the prison to them that are bound; To proclaim the acceptable year of the Lord, and the day of vengeance of our God; to comfort all that mourn; To appoint unto them that mourn in Zion, to give unto them beauty for ashes, the oil of joy for mourning, the garment of praise for the spirit of the heaviness; that they might be called trees of righteousness, the planting of the Lord, that he might be glorified.

Acknowledgements

First of all I want to say thank you to Jesus Christ our Savior. He is able to put back together broken hearts and dreams. He can give us peace, hope, and joy in every situation. He saves our soul and gives us a sound mind. There is no way to thank Him for all He has done. Without Him, life lacks meaning and direction. I know I am nothing without Him. I thank Him for the inspiration to write this book, and the opportunity to share what I have learned with others in similar situations. I am thankful that sin, circumstances, and failures didn't destroy me. He has somehow turned these things around to my advantage. Through them He has enabled me to accomplish my dream of writing a book.

At the 2003 Wings Conference, I heard a message on personality disorders. It was the first time I had heard anyone speak on this subject. The subject caught my interest because of the fact that I had been diagnosed with bipolar mood disorder and panic disorder in the past. It was Gayla Foster's message that inspired the writing of this book. I want to thank Gayla Foster for her inspiration, honesty, encouragement, referral to sources, and for her endorsement of this book. I also want to thank my daughter Sherry Cornejo for proofreading the manuscript, my family and friends for their prayers and encouragement, and MyLinn Sawyer and Brittany De La Cruz for the IBM Think Pad that has enabled me to work in my own home. Also, I want to thank Anne Suarez for her advice regarding self-publishing and Joanne's Putnam's book, *So You want to write*. I cannot forget to acknowledge Janice Owens, my college Instructor and friend, who took the time to have material transferred from Macintosh to IBM. I am thankful for the excellent work that Ana Mata did designing the cover for this book, and the time she sacrificed. You and many others not named have helped to make this book possible. Last but not least, I want to thank my Pastor and his wife, Ric and Vicki Gonzalez, for being an example of Christ in my life. They have helped me in so many ways. They have helped me to become who I am in Christ. I appreciate them both along with their children, Ricci, Ryan, and Elizabeth. I want to thank my Pastor for taking the time to write the forward, proofread, and advise me on the manuscript. Also, for his help in promoting this book. He has helped make publication of this work possible. My Pastor and his family have been one of God's greatest blessings to me.

My Desire

To have you, to know you, to seek your face.

You have given me my own special place.

You hear me cry out in my time of despair.

Your ear is attentive to every prayer.

With you by my side, I can do anything at all.

With my mind stayed on you, I won't stumble or fall.

If I listen to your voice, refusing every negative thought,

I can overcome the enemy's onslaught.

My desire is to go forth with your power and love,

Taking a message of deliverance from heaven above.

To those who are bound in prisons of the mind,

To thoughts of events that have them bound up by time.

Bound up by wounds of years gone past.

Chains of bondage that keep them in the enemy's grasp.

Lord, you can sever every tie that binds,

Give back to them control of their minds.

Introduction

We live in a society where it is difficult to keep up with the demands of everyday living, and it seems that things are moving faster all the time. Prices are going up constantly. Schedules are demanding, and many mothers are required to work. It is difficult to keep house, take care of children, and hold a job. Life can also be stressful for mothers who stay home all day taking care of children and household responsibilities. The fact that our country is at war is traumatic for many. They are fearful and unsure of what the outcome will be.

Dealing with the same daily schedule, and the same situations all the time can cause depression to set in. People lose hope, and begin to believe that things will never be different. Peter R. Breggin, M. D., and David Cohen, P.H.D., whom have over forty years of combined experience in the area of psychiatric drugs and are co-authors of the book, ***Your Drug May be Your Problem***, make the following statement regarding psychiatric drugs:

Psychiatric drugs are much more dangerous than many consumers and even physicians realize. All of these drugs produce numerous serious and potentially fatal adverse reactions, and most are capable of causing withdrawal problems that are emotionally and physically distressing. Some produce powerful physical dependence and can cause life-threatening withdrawal problems.

Breggin and Cohen pose the following questions, along with giving us some valuable insight into the methods used by many to handle the problems associated with every day life:

What is our ultimate resource in dealing with the stress of everyday life? Where do we turn when we feel emotionally upset or despairing? Where do we go when life seems unendurable and we have little or no hope left? What are our ultimate resources in life—the places and persons to whom we turn for help, direction, and inspiration? All people need faith, but the varieties of faith seem infinite. Increasingly, people nowadays turn to science to find answers about how to live life. Probably for most people, the final resort is a combination of resources: God, nature, science, other people, and oneself. Ultimately, all human resources are related. Commitment to a loving, zestful, rational, principled life becomes the cornerstone of life and the final resource. Many people, however, rely on another, more limited resource when they face psychological or social crisis. They turn to psychoactive or mind-altering substances. It appears that reliance on God, other people, and ourselves has been replaced with reliance on medical doctors and psychiatric drugs. The ultimate source of guidance and inspiration is no longer life itself with its infinite resources, but psychiatry with its narrow view of human nature. This view suggests that most if not all of our psychological, emotional, and spiritual problems are "psychiatric disorders" best treated by specialists who prescribe psychoactive drugs. (1-4)

Although they may believe or hope that they are relying on seemingly objective science, in reality they are placing their faith in drug company marketing—and so are their doctors. This point is worth underscoring: Physicians and even key health policy planners do not have access to all the necessary data required to make an independent evaluation of a drug's safety. They must instead rely on very general information provided by the FDA, which in turn relies largely on the drug companies themselves. FDA records contain thousands of severe and life-threatening reactions to almost every psychiatric drug in current use (102).

Consider the seemingly different situation with respect to recreational or illicit drugs. For untold millions throughout the world, the last resort is alcohol, tobacco, or substances such as marijuana and cocaine. Many turn to them when they are on the verge of experiencing painful emotions. In the extreme, they become addicted to these substances and build their lives around them. If people do feel better when drinking alcohol or smoking marijuana, it is because they feel better when their brain is impaired. Psychiatric drugs are no different. The people who take such drugs may feel less of their emotional suffering. They may even reach a state of relative anesthesia. But to the degree that they feel better, is because they are experiencing intoxication with the drugs (1-2).

Many people with emotional problems will visit a psychiatrist who will diagnose the way they are feeling as a chemical imbalance. According to Breggin and Cohen, the chemicals in the brain cannot be measured:

The human brain has more individual cells (neurons) than there are stars in the sky. Billions! And each neuron may have 10,000 or more connections (synapses) to other brain cells, creating a network with trillions of interconnections. In fact, the brain is considered to be the most complex organ in the entire universe. Scientists have well-developed ideas about how the physical universe works. They possess mathematical formulae for describing the various forces that control the relationships among physical entities from black holes to subatomic particles. All these forces also affect the human brain. However, the living processes of the brain add complexities unknown in the physical universe. There are trillions of interconnections between brain cells. These interconnections are mediated by hundreds of chemical messengers, (neurotransmitters), as well as by hormones, proteins, and tiny ions such as sodium and potassium, and other substances. We have limited knowledge about how a few of these chemical messengers work, but little or no idea as to how they combine to produce brain function.
The public is told that a great deal of science is involved in the prescription of psychiatric drugs, but this is not so—given that we know so little about how the brain works. The knowledge that we do have about the effects of psychiatric drugs on the brain is largely limited to test-tube studies of biochemical reactions

utilizing ground-up pieces of animal brain. We simply do not understand the overall impact of the drugs on the brain. Nor do we have a clear idea about the relationship between brain function and mental phenomena such as "mood" or "emotions" like depression or anxiety. We don't even know where to begin looking because we don't fully understand how the brain functions (5).

Based on these facts, and more that will be presented, we can conclude that there are no medical or scientific findings to prove that depression or anxiety is caused by chemical imbalances:

Some theoreticians would urge us to focus on the molecular level by looking for biochemical imbalances. But that is sheer speculation. Why would a biochemical imbalance be at the root of feeling very depressed any more that it would be at the root of feeling very happy? And if there were biochemical substrates for extreme sadness and extreme happiness, would that in fact make them diseases? The idea of individual biochemical imbalances is wholly at odds with the complexity of the brain. Besides, whose biochemical imbalance are we looking for? That of the child who is out of control or that of the caregiver who has difficulty disciplining? That of the child who isn't learning or the teacher who hasn't figured out how to reach this child? That of the individual who becomes anxious in dealing with people or the adult that abused the individual as a child? That of the person who is deeply depressed over a lost loved one or the doctor who recommends electroshock? That of the person who feels insecure or anxious or the doctor who thinks that the person's problem requires drugs? In short, whose brain isn't working right? As one of our colleagues recently said, "Biochemical imbalances are the only diseases spread by word of mouth". (Breggin and Cohen 6)

Bipolar mood disorder and panic disorder are theorized to be the result of a chemical imbalance. These disorders are commonly treated with antidepressants and anti-anxiety drugs such as Zoloft, Prozac, Paxal, Wellbutrin, Valium, Ativan, and Xanax. Breggin and Cohen make these statements regarding the administration of psychoactive drugs for depression and anxiety:

Individually, we must all use our own intuitive understanding of life to determine the likelihood that our problems are caused by some as-yet-undetected brain dysfunction rather than by conflicts in the home, at work, society, painful life experiences, confused values, a lack of direction, or other aspects of human life. Of course, our bodies can affect our emotional out look. We all find it much easier to maintain a bright and enthusiastic attitude when physically healthy than when physically ill. And anything from lack of sleep to the common cold can affect our moods. However, doctors commonly give people psychiatric drugs without checking for the obvious signs of a serious physical disorder, such as hypothyroidism, estrogen deficiency, or head injury from a car accident. Moreover, they seem particularly prone to overlooking the importance of physical symptoms in women. Some women with obvious signs of a hormonal disease or heart condition are put on antidepressants and anti-anxiety drugs without first being required by their internists or psychiatrists to undergo a physical evaluation. It is therefore theoretically possible that some anxious or depressed people may be afflicted with an as-yet-undetected physical dysfunction. But this speculation doesn't justify the unfounded conclusion that people in emotional distress are beset by specific biochemical imbalances or that such imbalances can be corrected with drugs (6-7). It should be noted that hormone imbalance has been known to substantially affect mood and emotions in some individuals.

Based on years of experience, Breggin and Cohen make the following statements regarding individuals who suffer with depression:

Most people with depression and anxiety have obvious reasons for how they feel. These reasons are often apparent in their everyday lives and may be complicated by past experiences in childhood or earlier adult life. Most of all psychiatric drug research is done on the normal brains of animals, usually rats. As noted earlier, much of this research involves grinding up the brain tissues to investigate the gross effects of a drug on one or more limited biochemical reactions in the brain. More sophisticated research involves micro-instrumentation that injects small amounts of drugs into the living brain and measures the firing of cells. Yet even these more refined methods are gross compared to the actual molecular level in the brain. For example, we have no techniques for measuring the actual levels of neurotransmitters in the synapses between the cells. Thus all talk about biochemical imbalances is pure guesswork. More important, what's actually being studied is the disruption of normal processes by the intrusion of foreign substances. This research in no way bolsters the idea that psychiatric drugs correct imbalances. Rather, it shows that psychiatric drugs create imbalances. In modern psychiatric treatment, we take the single most complicated known creation in the universe—the human brain—and pour drugs into it in the hope of "improving" its function when in reality we are disrupting its function. The notion that Prozac corrects biochemical imbalances is sheer speculation—propaganda from the biological psychiatric industry (7).

Research has proven that psychoactive drugs can be disruptive and harmful to normal brain function:

Taking drugs causes disruption of biochemical reactions in the brain. This causes severe biochemical imbalances and abnormal rates of firing among brain cells. This is a proven fact about Prozac that cannot honestly be disputed by anyone who knows the research. The brain reacts to psychoactive drugs as if being invaded by toxic substances; it tries to overcome, or compensate for, the harmful drug effects. In the process the brain literally destroys it own capacity to respond to the drug. It numbs itself and in doing so, actually kills some of its own functions. So when a doctor tells us that Prozac is putting our biochemicals into balance, we are being badly misled. In actuality, Prozac is profoundly disrupting the function of the brain. We already know that the brain's recovery from exposure to many psychiatric drugs may be prolonged and full recovery may never take place. We also know that irreversible changes can occur in response to the drugs used to treat schizophrenia, such as Haldol, Proxilin, and Risperdal. These drugs can cause permanent, severe, impairments of brain function (8-9).

The following analogy paints a frightening picture of what we are doing to our brains if we put our faith in psychoactive drugs:

Imagine if we treated our much simpler computers the same way we treat the brain in psychiatry. Consider the case of a computer that is "crashing" too often. With considerable poetic license, we can compare this mechanical dysfunction to the human tendency to become "overwhelmed" or "overloaded" with depression, anxiety, or obsessions and compulsions, and unable to function easily in everyday life. Perhaps the computer is crashing for reasons having to do this its hardware. For example, the computer may need more memory or a new hard drive. Alternatively, the problem may be traceable to its software—to one or more of the programs installed in the computer. Then again the operator of the computer and its programs may be responsible. Or the source of the problem could lie outside of the computer and even outside of the office, as in the case of power surges. When trouble shooting such a problem, the computer experts routinely take all of these factors into consideration—the computer, the program, the operator, and the power source. If the cause of the problem isn't immediately apparent, they may run experimental tests or programs in order to diagnose the problem. The approach taken by psychiatrists and other medical doctors, by contrast, is both simple-minded and destructive. In contemporary psychiatry, the doctor almost always assumes that problem lies in the "hardware" of the brain (i.e. "biochemical imbalances"). Modern psychiatrists seem to consider themselves brain consultants, but they have little knowledge with which to establish that expertise. Unlike computer consultants, psychiatrists have no way of identifying or locating the source of the problem in a patient's brain. So the patient must take their "expert" assertions on faith. How would you react if your computer consultant treated your computer the way psychiatrists treat patients and their brains? Suppose your consultant invariably concluded that the problem must lie in the hardware of your machine rather than the program, the operator, or some external factor such as the power source. Suppose your consultant always began by pouring toxic agents into your computer. Further more, suppose that your consultant never guaranteed you a good result while continuing to pour toxic agents into your machine. Without any regard for the consequences—and, when pressed for an explanation, made vague references to "crossed wires" or "electrical imbalances" in your computer but never looked inside, conducted and tests, or provided a definite diagnosis. How long would you put up with such nonsense from your computer consultant? If computer consultants behaved like psychiatrists, we would fire them. Yet, tens of millions of people put up with even more slipshod, irrational treatments involving their far more complex and vulnerable brains and minds. (Breggin and Cohen 9-10)

It should be noted at this point that this book is intended to deal strictly with emotional and spiritual conditions. I want to make it **clear** that I am **not** saying we shouldn't take medication or see a physician when we are physically ill. Also, there are times when an infirmity in an individual's brain will cause behavioral problems, an example would be a brain tumor. In cases like these we should seek the help of a physician, but we must remember that Jesus is our healer. The medications discussed in this book are psychoactive drugs that affect the mind.

This book was written to make the reader aware of the hope we have in Jesus Christ. If we look to His word, we will find an answer to every problem. Jesus came to speak the gospel of good news into our lives, open the prison doors, heal the broken hearted, comfort those who mourn, give us beauty for ashes, and so much more. He gives us these things with no harmful side effects.

It is my hope and prayer that this book will give scriptural solutions to spiritual problems. The word of God can enter the human soul and spirit, and repair things that the medical field can't. Hebrews 4:12 says **"For the word of God is quick, and powerful, and sharper than any two-edged sword, piercing even to the dividing asunder of soul and spirit, and of the**

joints and marrow, and is a discerner of the thoughts and intents of the heart."

The word of God is a living force. The Greek translation for the word quick is "alive". The word of God can touch our heart and minds. It can cut to the heart of spiritual problems, and change negative views to positive ones. It has the power to convict us, and it can save our soul because it can heal our mind.

I heard a story from a reputable source about a man who was insane. He was living in a mental institution. One day someone brought him a Bible, and he began to read it. Reading the word of God began a healing process in his mind. The story ended with the man leaving the institution.

The word of God never changes, but God's word is alive. Therefore, it has the power to reveal itself to us in a way that enables it to minister to different needs in our lives at different times. If we are experiencing a trial in our lives, we can read a scripture we have read before, and it will give us new revelation, hope, or confirmation in our time of need. Medication will not help us overcome depression or stress. Jesus has a better way for us. He is our hope in every situation. Jesus is the solid rock we can stand on. Medication may temporarily help because it desensitizes us to the matter at hand. We can drink a shot of whiskey and get the same results. Neither will solve the problem because the problem is never dealt with.

I want to encourage those who feel they have no course of action to take other than modern psychology. I want to testify that there is a better way, and I have learned it from personal experience. Jesus is the great physician. He doesn't charge for an office call, and His counsel is free. You don't need health insurance. All it takes is willingness, effort on the part of an individual, and a relationship with Jesus Christ to be made whole. He is available every minute of the day. He is our counselor, and He wants to be our best friend. He is a friend that sticks closer than a brother.

The Bible says in Isaiah 9:6, **"For unto us a child is born, unto us a son is given: and the government shall be upon his shoulder: and his name shall be called Wonderful, Counsellor, The mighty God, The everlasting Father, The Prince of Peace."** Isaiah 9:7 tells us that the increase of His government, and His peace will never end. Colossians 2:9 tells us that the fullness of the Godhead is in the body of Jesus Christ. Colossians 2:10 tells us that we are complete in Him, and that He is the head of all power and principalities. All divine power and governmental authority has been given to Jesus Christ forever. He has the ability to overcome any principality, heal any disease, forgive any sin, pronounce judgement against anyone, and overthrow any kingdom. He is all we need to become whole, and be delivered from the damaging effects of sin in our lives.

I thank Him for His delivering power. I lived 38 years bound by depression, fear, shame, bitterness, rebellion, drugs, and alcohol. I can remember not wanting to wake up in the morning because I didn't want to face the day. This was damaging to my children, and I was not the mother they deserved. I was involved in an abusive marriage that didn't last. I used alcohol and drugs hoping they would make me feel different, but in the end I only felt worse. I get angry at the devil when I think of the deception, the wasted years of my life, and the needless suffering of my children. For this cause, I come against satan's evil works every day in the name of Jesus.

The devil has been attempting to destroy families for thousands of years. Because we are at the end of the age, this activity has accelerated the past few decades. Television and other sources clearly reveal that he is working hard in his attempt to desensitize us to sin. He is attempting to make sin seem acceptable. Every program has subject matter that goes against the word of God. Also, it is not uncommon to see drugs for depression, and ADHD advertised as if they were aspirin. Remember that one of satan's main goals is to destroy our children. Perhaps that is why I want to fight him like I do. The best way to fight him is with the truth. He is a liar and a murderer. He has been since the beginning. We can be confident in knowing he will have his place in the lake of fire.

After years of living with depression, I went to a psychiatrist when I was approximately 30 years old. The psychiatrist diagnosed me with bipolar mood disorder, and prescribed a drug called Zoloft. This medication increased the feeling of fear, and nervousness I already felt. When I told the psychiatrist I felt this way, he prescribed Valium for panic disorder. I was soon taking more Valium than prescribed because the dose I was on did not eliminate the fear I felt.

Eventually, I was hospitalized for addiction to Valium. I was then put on an anti-convulsant drug called Tegretol. I was still prescribed Zoloft as well. These drugs had many side effects, and never improved my condition. Drugs didn't solve the problem because sin and the absence of God in my life were its cause. Since the drugs didn't improve the way I felt, I continued to use alcohol along with them.

I finally decided to stop taking the drugs before the mixture of drugs and alcohol killed me. When I informed the psychiatrist of my decision, I was told I could have seizures. The doctor advised me to stay on the medication. I ignored his advice, and began to wean myself gradually off the medication until I ran out. During my last visit to the psychiatrist, he gave me some sample boxes of Zoloft. He said, "take these in case you crash." I was still depressed, but I was glad to be rid of the side effects of the drugs. The effect these drugs had on my life will be further discussed in the following text.

Before knowing Jesus, nothing ever changed the way I felt. Even the things I was involved in that weren't destructive brought only temporary happiness, but never true joy. Happiness is something this world offers, but it is conditional. Happiness is based on circumstances, but peace and joy only come from the kingdom of God. They remain during hard times and bad circumstances. I can honestly say I never knew joy until I received the Holy Ghost and was baptized in Jesus name.

Before I came into the Church, I had given up hope that things could ever be different. I didn't realize when I received the Holy Ghost and was baptized in the name of Jesus for the remission of my sins that it was only the beginning. I had just begun my walk in the newness of life. After I was born again,

Jesus enabled me to begin a process of conversion by changing my way of thinking. He has enabled me to establish a lifestyle of prayer and fasting, and has given me the ability to extend forgiveness to others. It is my prayer as I write this book that it will give hope to those who read it. I pray in the name of Jesus that the reader will feel the hope, peace, and joy that only Jesus can give. I dedicate this book to every individual who wants deliverance, and has the mind to allow God to change their present circumstances. To those who are willing to take the measure of faith God has given them, and apply the principles in the word of God to their lives. I pray in the name of Jesus that they will receive the deliverance the Lord has for them. There is deliverance for all that seek and desire it.

The Shepherd

For every lost sheep, you make a way.

None are forgotten, you see them stray.

Every path you direct and facilitate,

You open the door at the pearly gate.

There's only one way, one road to you.

Our ways are flawed,

Your word will see us through.

We need you to guide us, to show us the way.

To have and to seek you, your word we obey.

You are the good shepherd, you have given all.

You came to the world, in spite of its flaws.

Looking for the lost, for souls to keep.

To rescue from darkness, to wake those who sleep.

For those who think there is no better way,

To awaken, enlighten, empower to pray.

To be with us always, to straighten our ways.

To lead us through life, to take us home one day.

In Loving Memory

Of

David Allen Fultz

August 17, 1960 – January 5, 2005

Chapter One

The Opening of the Prison Doors to Them That are Bound

Jesus spoke to His disciples before ascending into heaven saying, **"...that repentance and remission of sins should be preached in his name among all nations, beginning at Jerusalem" (Luke 24:47).** This scripture is relevant to us today. These words Jesus spoke are the key to unlocking the invisible prison doors of the mind. The prison doors of our mind will open when we realize we need deliverance, and are willing to receive it. In order to receive deliverance and salvation, we must be willing to repent of the way we have been living. To repent means to **turn away from sin** towards God.

A Jewish leader named Nicodemus came to Jesus by night to learn more from Him. **"Jesus answered him...Verily, verily, I say unto to thee, Expect a man be born again, he cannot see the kingdom of God" (John 3:3).** Nicodemus asked Jesus, how can a man reenter his mother's womb and be born again? **"Jesus answered, Verily, Verily, I say unto thee, Expect a man be born of the water and the spirit, he cannot enter into the kingdom of God" (John 3:5).**

According to these scriptures, there are two requirements given by Jesus for entering the kingdom of God. If we search the New Testament scriptures, we discover that water baptism fulfills the first part of the requirement given by Jesus. Water baptism signifies a death to our old nature, and washing away of past sin. Colossians 2:12 says we are buried with Him in baptism, and resurrected by the power of God.

In Colossians 2:11-13, the Apostle Paul used New Testament baptism as an analogy to Old Testament circumcision. Paul said that baptism is a circumcision performed without hands to subdue our fleshly nature that leads to sin. This is accomplished by putting on the nature of Christ. Paul told the Jews in Romans 2:29 that circumcision of their flesh didn't make them Jews, but one must be a Jew inwardly. He said that circumcision of the heart and spirit is what pleases God. We must make every effort to conquer our corrupt nature, and be renewed by the nature of Christ.

The word baptism comes from the Greek word 'baptizo', and means to dunk, immerse or soak. Water baptism by immersion is required for the remission of sins. Acts 2:38 says, **"Repent, and be baptized every one of you in the name of Jesus Christ for the remission of sins, and ye shall receive the gift of the Holy Ghost."** The word remission translated to the Greek language means pardon, deliverance, forgiveness, and liberty.

When our sins are remitted by baptism, we are free from the debt of our past sin. Without baptism, the blood that washes away sin has not been applied. Hebrews 10:1-4 tells us that the law contained a shadow of the good things to come, but it was impossible for the blood of animals to take away sin. So God provided a better sacrifice. The people had to offer sacrifices year after year, but these never cleared their conscience. God became the perfect sacrifice for all time that we might receive justification through our faith in Jesus Christ.

Baptism is a commandment that represents the fulfillment of a blood covenant between man and God. Baptism is a commandment given under the New Covenant that involves a circumcision of the heart. God did away with the law that required circumcision of the flesh, and replaced it with a law that involves the condition of our heart. The condition of our heart is what God is concerned about. When our heart is right with God, we will have a desire to do what is right. The scribes and Pharisees, who were the religious leaders of His day, came to question Jesus because His disciples did not follow the tradition of washing their hands before they ate (see Matthew 15:1-2).

Jesus responded to their accusation by calling them hypocrites. He told them that they had overlooked the commandments of God, and replaced His commandments with their traditions. Then He spoke the prophecy of Isaiah saying, **"This people draweth nigh unto me with their mouth, and honoureth me with their lips; but their heart is far from me. But in vain they do worship me, teaching for doctrines the commandments of men" (Matthew 15:8-9).** Paul warned the Church about following the doctrines of men in Colossians 2:8, saying, **"Beware lest any man spoil you through Philosophy and vain deceit, after the tradition of men, after the rudiments of the world, and not after Christ."** We must have a love for truth and have a desire in our hearts to know the righteous and holy God who created us.

Jesus told the multitudes about the importance of a having a clean heart. He said, **"Not that which goeth into the mouth defileth a man; but that which commeth out of the mouth, this defileth a man. For out of the heart proceed evil thoughts, murders, adulteries, fornications, thefts, false witness, blasphemies: These are the things which defile a man: but to eat with unwashen hands defileth not a man" (Matthew 15:11, 19-20).** Jesus teaches us through these scriptures that God is very concerned about the condition of our heart. God is the only one who sees our heart and knows our thoughts (see I Kings 8:39). If we are to live righteous and holy lives we must begin by changing the way we think. We must search for truth in God's word, not in the doctrines of men. God's word is true, and His word is our connection with the mind of God. Jesus said that if we continue in His word, we are His disciples. He also said that we will know the truth, and the truth will make us free (see John 8:31-32).

King David asked God in Psalm 19:14, **"Let the words of my mouth, and the meditation of my heart, be acceptable in thy sight, O Lord, my strength, and my redeemer."** We must meditate on the word of God and put away all evil and deceptive thoughts. We cannot dwell on these types of things. Evil or untrue thoughts, if they are dwelt upon, will eventually produce evil actions. These types of thoughts include anything that is against what scripture teaches us. These thoughts will cause us to say and do things that are wrong. Jesus said, **"out of the**

abundance of the heart the mouth speaks" (see Matthew 12:34). When we set our minds on pure thoughts and desire to do what is right, it will show in our speech and actions.

The Bible tells us that John the Baptist baptized Jesus. John didn't feel that he was worthy to baptize Jesus. But Jesus told John that He must be baptized in order for all righteousness to be fulfilled (See Matthew 3:15). As long as we live on this earth we will battle with our fallen nature, but we can achieve a level of righteousness that will enable us to rise above sin. Jesus was baptized for our example, and He was without sin. Therefore, we should see the need to have our sins remitted, as the scripture teaches us, to fulfill righteousness in our lives. Water Baptism in the name of Jesus enables us to become people of His name. Baptism in the name of Jesus applies the blood of Jesus to our lives. Baptism as a means for salvation has always been in the mind of God. The instructions given to the New Testament Church can be seen in Old Testament typology. We see a type of water baptism when God instructed Moses to have the sons of Aaron wash in a brasen laver before they ministered and offered sacrifices (see Exodus 30:18-21).

I Peter 3:20-21 compares water baptism to the salvation Noah's family received, baptism being a like figure of the eight souls saved by water. When God's people were delivered from the bondage of Egypt, the death angel passed over all the houses that had blood applied to the post of the doors. The Passover is still celebrated by the Jews unto this day. The blood applied during the Passover represents deliverance from death and salvation (see Exodus 12:5-13). God told His people,

"when I see the blood, I will pass over you, and the plague will not destroy you."

According to Mark 1:9-10, John 3:23, Acts 8:38-39, Romans 6:4-5, Acts 2:38, Acts 8:16, Acts 10:47-48, Acts 19:4-5, Acts 22:16, Romans 6:3-4, I Corinthians 1:12-15, Galatians 3:27, and Colossians 2:11-12, baptism was always performed by immersion in the name of Jesus. This was the only way the apostles baptized. They were commissioned by God to do so. In order to see signs, wonders, and captives set free, we must do as the apostles did. We can't add or subtract from the word of God.

The second requirement for entering the Kingdom of God given by Jesus was to be born again of the spirit. Our spirit is reborn when we receive the Holy Ghost. Speaking in other tongues is the evidence of this rebirth. Acts 2:4 says **"And they were all filled with the Holy Ghost, and began to speak with other tongues, as the Spirit gave them utterance."** It was prophesied in Isaiah 28:11, **"For with stammering lips and another tongue will he speak to this people."** The prophet Joel prophesied that in the last days God would pour out His spirit on all flesh. This prophecy began to be fulfilled on the day of Pentecost (see Acts 2:1-4).

God's spirit enables us to rise above sin and its consequences. It is God's desire to repair the breach caused by sin, and communicate with His most treasured creation. When we receive the Holy Ghost, we become God's habitation. We are His hands, His feet, and His voice in this world. The second Adam, who came in the form of Jesus Christ as the image of the invisible God, repaired the damage caused by the first Adam. The Bible tells us in Isaiah 53:6 and II Corinthians 5:21, that our iniquity was laid on Him and He became sin for us. I Corinthians 15:55-57 says that He has given us the power to have victory over sin and death.

Speaking in other tongues is more than speaking in a language we don't understand. Speaking in other tongues is a sign that someone has received the Holy Ghost, and is a witness to the unbeliever. Speaking with other tongues is God's chosen method to open a door of lost communication with mankind. Communication was lost when sin entered the Garden of Eden (see Genesis 3:24). When God created Adam and Eve, he communed with them everyday in the garden. Sin caused a breach between man and God, and according to Romans 8:2, sin also brought death.

Jesus is our only hope to overcome sin and death. Romans 5:14 says, **"Nevertheless death reigned from Adam to Moses, even over them that had not sinned after the similitude of Adam's transgression, who was the like figure of him that was to come. Romans 5:19 says, "For as by one man's disobedience many were made sinners, so by the obedience of one shall many be made righteous."** The Bible also tells us in Romans 5:21 that grace reigns through righteousness. We must make an attempt to live righteously in order for grace to reign in our lives. Since we all have a fallen nature, we need divine assistance to help us subdue the works of our flesh.

God's Spirit enables us to live above sin. The word Holy translated back to the Greek is pure, blameless, consecrated. When the word Ghost is translated to Greek, the meaning is God, Christ's Spirit or Mind. It is a powerful thing to have the Spirit of the living God dwelling within us. The Bible calls the Holy Ghost the Comforter and the Spirit of truth. The Holy Ghost will help us discern what is right or wrong, and keep us from being deceived by false doctrine. John 16:13 tells us that the Spirit of truth will guide us into all truth. The Holy Ghost will also help us overcome our human faults and weaknesses. It should be noted that the gift of the Holy Ghost (Acts 2:38) is not the same as the gift of tounges (I Corinthians 12:10).

The baptism of the Holy Ghost is for everyone, not just for certain individuals. The gift of tounges is a spiritual gift that works through the power of the Holy Ghost. Jesus gives us an example of those who are born of the Spirit. **"The wind bloweth where it listeth, and thou hearest the sound thereof, but canst not tell whence it cometh, and wither it goeth: so is every one that is born of the spirit" (John 3:8).** We can hear the wind, but we can't see where it comes from or where it goes. In the same sense we cannot see God's spirit, but we can hear sound to indicate that someone has been born of the spirit. The word sound used in this scripture comes from the Greek word "fon-nay". This is where we get the word phone in the English language. This word means, saying, language, noise, sound, or voice. Jesus gives us this example so we may understand that when someone is born of the spirit, an audible sound will be heard.

Jesus also said that unless we are converted, and become like little children, we shall not enter the kingdom of heaven (see Matthew 18:3). To be born again of the water and the spirit is only the beginning. After we are born again, a conversion process must take place. True conversion means a change of heart that will show in the way we think and act. Conversion requires a combination of our will and God's power. We must choose to allow the measure of God's character given to us by the Holy Ghost to change us. The literal meaning of the word converted is to turn around, to turn self about. It is up to us to choose to walk in our new nature, and not revert back to our old sinful nature.

The word children means child, infant, half-grown boy or girl, or immature Christian. We must be willing to humble ourselves to God and others. We mustn't be haughty, proud, or rebellious. We must have childlike faith, believing in our Heavenly Father as a child believes in their earthly parents. We must be willing to help others when there is a need. Children are quick to forgive, and anxious to help with everything. Sometimes they will even argue over who will be allowed to help. Remember, we must be childlike not childish. Above all else, we must love and believe the word of God. Our conversion is one of the most powerful things we have. It is our testimony, and it shows others the awesome power of God.

The word of God is the most powerful force that exists. Psalm 138:2 says, **"...for thou hast magnified thy word above all thy name."** The word of God is forever settled in heaven, and cannot be moved. The Bible tells us that the word is God, and the word became flesh, and dwelt among us (see John 1:1, 14). The previous scriptures tell us that Jesus is the word of God. Without obedience to the word of God, it is impossible to receive salvation. God and His word are one, and we must believe that all scripture was God inspired (see II Timothy 3:16).

Some believe that scripture was written based on the thoughts or will of man. Some believe there are different interpretations of scripture. According to the Bible, these statements are not true. In fact, Peter says the first thing we should know is that there are no private interpretations of scripture. The word private implies pertaining to self or ones own. The Bible tells us, **"Knowing this first, that no prophecy of the scripture is of any private interpretation. For the prophecy came not in old time by the will of man: but holy men of God spake as they were moved by the Holy Ghost" (II Peter 1:20-21).**

The written word of God is our foundation. If we don't believe the word, we have no foundation to stand on. However, it is possible to have knowledge of scripture without revelation. Revelation involves our human will. Past traditions we have been taught can blind us to the truth. Our fleshly nature will not always want to go along with the righteous and holy nature of God. Therefore, we shouldn't attempt to bend God's word to our will, but we must change our will to conform to God's word. We will never change the written word of God. It's solid as a rock, and those who reject the word are rejecting Jesus. Jesus said in Luke 20:18, **"Whosoever shall fall upon that stone shall be**

broken; but on whomsoever it shall fall, it will grind him to powder." It is better to be broken and transformed into a new creature by the word of God than to be crushed to powder by it on judgement day.

We can't base what we believe on doctrines of men that don't agree with scripture. Paul warned Timothy that there would come a time when people would not have patience for sound doctrine. He said that they would seek teachers who will say what they want to hear, and what goes along with their lust of the flesh. In the end they will turn away from the truth, and be deceived into believing lies (see II Timothy 4:3-4). Things that sound good to our carnal nature don't benefit our spiritual man. Those who choose to follow teaching that caters to the lust of their flesh will be lead astray by false doctrine.

God has chosen to speak through man in order to reveal His plan for salvation, and His purpose for our lives. God chose Prophets and Apostles to record the inspired words spoken to them by God and their writings were preserved for all time. The Bible was written over a four thousand-year-period. The Bible includes Holy Ghost inspired writings from people of many different cultural and economic backgrounds. In spite of the time span between writings, and differences in the lives of the writers, no inconsistency can be found throughout scripture. These facts, along with God confirming His word with signs and wonders, give witness to the authenticity of scripture.

Anyone who desires to be a Christian must live according to the laws of God. The laws of the living God are found in the Bible. To overcome the adversary we must know, and follow

God's laws. God enables us to live by His laws by giving us His Spirit and His name. The Holy Ghost gives us the power to overcome sin, and baptism in Jesus name gives us the authority to overcome our adversary. We must decide what course of action we will take.

Today many people do not want to take responsibility for their own actions. Sometimes people will blame others or circumstances for their actions. It's part of human nature. We must decide human nature is not good enough, especially if it isn't working for us. We need God's nature. In order for God's nature to be formed in us, we must spend time with Him in prayer, and learn about Him by reading His word. Then we must put what we have read into action, and do our best to follow His word. **"But be ye doers of the word, and not hearers only, deceiving your own selves" (James 1:22).** Every word in scripture comes from the mind of God. His word is spirit and truth. To overcome, we must line up our thinking with His word. Change will only come when we take the necessary steps to bring it about.

Philippians 2:5 says, **"Let this mind be in you, which was also in Christ Jesus."** The word mind in the original Greek means mentally disposed, to interest oneself with concern of obedience, to set the affection on, to be of one, to be of the same. We know from reading about the life of Jesus that He was in total obedience to the word of God, and He certainly came with one purpose in mind. We are instructed to be like-minded in our purpose and intent. James 1:8 says, **"A double-minded man is unstable in all his ways."** To be double-minded implies that a person is two-spirited, and vacillates in opinion or purpose.

When we have the mind of Christ, we won't be swayed by every wind of doctrine, or deterred by every circumstance that arises. Our minds will be good ground where the word of God can grow and produce. Those who intentionally violate the word of God will eventually be turned over to a reprobate mind. Romans 1:28 tells us, **"And even as they did not like to retain God in their knowledge, God gave them over to a reprobate mind, to do those things which are not convenient."** In this scripture, the Greek translation of the word mind is the intellect, divine or human in thought, feeling, will, and understanding. The meaning of the word reprobate is unapproved, rejected or castaway. If someone has been turned over to a reprobate mind, it is because they have willfully gone against the truth that has been revealed to them. God has turned them over to their own will, and they have become deceived and blinded to the truth. A reprobate mind will produce actions that are against the laws of God and man.

There are many aspects to the human mind. It is not a physical organ like the brain. The mind can't be seen or examined by scientists or psychiatrists. With the help of modern technology, the brain can be seen and operated on. The medical field doesn't have this ability with the mind because it is hidden from human eyes. However, it is evident that our will and ambitions are controlled by our minds. In scripture the mind and soul are synonymous. The Greek translation of the word soul is heart, life, and mind. Jesus is the only one that can renew our mind, and save our soul. The Bible says we are made up of body, soul, and spirit (see I Thessalonians 5:23). Obviously it is not possible for our soul or spirit to become physically ill. The brain can become diseased because it is part of our physical body, but spiritual problems that involve our thinking cannot be treated with medication.

Damage to our soul and spirit can occur as a result of sin, traumatic experiences, or sin committed against us by others. Jesus is the only one who can heal our mind, and it is His will to do so. We limit God's ability to heal us by trusting in science to heal our spiritual problems. When Jesus was asked why He spoke in parables, He spoke the words of the prophet Isaiah (see Isaiah 6:10). **"For this people's heart is waxed gross, and their ears are dull of hearing, and their eyes they have closed; lest at any time they should see with their eyes, and hear with their ears, and should understand with their heart, and should be converted, and I should heal them" (Matthew 13:15).** Is it possible that Jesus spoke in parables to test men's hearts? The hungry heart will seek after God until the answer is found. We need to open our eyes to God's word, and our ears to His voice. If we will search the scriptures for an answer, and seek God's truth when we are tormented in our minds, we can be forever changed.

Jesus is the only one who can heal the effects of sin on our lives. It doesn't matter what has happened in the past, or what disorder someone has been diagnosed with. Jesus has the power to heal if we have a desire to be healed by Him. Matthew 4:24 says, **"And his fame went throughout all Syria: and**

they brought unto him all sick people that were taken with divers diseases and torments, and those which were possessed with devils, and those which were lunatic, and those that had the palsy; and he healed them." The Bible says great multitudes followed Jesus. They believed that He could heal them. Many had to walk a long way to find Jesus, and He always had compassion on them. He healed them, and fed them when they were hungry. What is stopping us from seeking Him for our needs today? He hasn't changed.

When we are born again, making every effort to align our lives with His word, we will receive more of the mind of Christ. This means we will be lead by His spirit, His word, and His voice. This is a continuing process, which will bring about mature Christianity in our lives. As long as we live we will keep growing in Him. After starting Churches and doing a great work for God, the Apostle Paul said, **"Not as though I had already attained, either were already perfect: but I follow after, if that I may apprehend that for which also I am apprehended of Christ Jesus" (Philippians 3:12).**

If we love Him, we will make every effort to follow Him and obey His commandments instead of being conformed to worldly things. The Bible says, **"And be not conformed to this world: but be ye transformed by the renewing of your mind, that ye may prove what is that good, and acceptable, and perfect, will of God" (Romans 12:2).** In order to find the perfect will of God for us, we must change the way we think. We must renew our minds and be willing to break old thought patterns. It is not the will of God for anyone to be on mind altering drugs. It is not

His will for anyone to be bound by depression or any other mental problem. Matthew 4:24 says that He healed everyone no matter what was wrong with them. It is His desire to deliver us from every kind of torment. The faith of the people in Matthew 4:24 made their healing and deliverance possible.

Once we are delivered, a relationship with Him keeps us delivered. The Bible says in Matthew 4:25, that after He healed the people, great multitudes followed Him. Also, a man that Jesus delivered from demon possession wanted to follow Him (see Mark 5:18). Those people knew Jesus had something they needed beyond healing and deliverance. It is not enough to be delivered. We need a relationship with Jesus to be transformed, develop the mind of Christ, and stay delivered. The only way we can know Jesus personally is to spend time with Him in prayer and read His word. It is impossible to get to know anyone you don't spend time talking to. The Bible tells us that without holiness we cannot see God. In order to become holy, we must spend time in the presence of the One who is holy. Prayer and the word are our foundation, but our human will determines if we receive God's instruction.

Also, we must control the influences that come into our minds everyday. King David said he would put no wicked thing before his eyes (See Psalm 101:3). We must consider what we watch and read each day. We must also be in control of the things we allow our minds to dwell on. Our thoughts, if we dwell on them long enough, will become our actions. This is true whether the thoughts are good or bad, so let's dwell on what's good. Since Jesus tells us only God is good, the best thing we can do is dwell on Him.

When we pray and fill our mind with His word, we begin to see things the way God sees them. **"For who hath known the mind of the Lord, that he may instruct him? But we have the mind Christ" (I Corinthians 2:16).** In order for Him to instruct us, we must be willing to pray and receive His counsel. When we don't pray or read His word, our carnal mind will take over. When this happens we have a problem. The enemy of our soul will introduce thoughts into our mind that are not of God. Our mind is the war zone where our salvation will be won or lost.

When we pray and know the word, we will be able to resist the voice of the enemy. When we don't do these things, we become carnally minded. The Bible tells us a carnal mind is opposed to God and His laws. **"Because the carnal mind is enmity against God: for it is not subject to the law of God, neither indeed can be" (Romans 8:7).** The word enmity in the Greek language means hostility, opposition or hatred. The word carnal means the body as opposed to the soul or spirit. Our fleshy thinking is in direct opposition to the law of God.

This is why it is so important to be led by the spirit of God. We must remember our mind is subject to human nature with its frailties, (moral or physical), and passions. When we think carnally, not only are we in opposition to God, but we are also subject to frailty in thinking. If we aren't to be deceived by wrong thinking processes, we must learn to think in accordance with God's word and be led by His spirit. When we experience the same spiritual problems repeatedly, something is obviously wrong. Negative thoughts do not come from God, and must be continually cast down. We must remember everything about God is positive.

Negative thoughts towards ourselves come from shame and condemnation. These negative factors have control in our lives when we don't believe in God's love or desire to forgive us. If sin is involved, the Holy Ghost will convict us. He does this in order to extend mercy, and draw us to repentance. If we repent and don't feel forgiven, these feelings are a result of condemnation. God won't convict us of sin that has been repented of. The Bible tells us that, **"There is therefore now no condemnation to them which are in Christ Jesus, who walk not after the flesh, but after the spirit" (Romans 8:1).** When we are doing our best to turn from sin toward God, we can rest assured that all feelings of unworthiness are false condemnation.

We must believe Calvary has made us worthy and we must allow God to enable us to think with a sound mind. **"For God hath not given us the spirit of fear; but of power, and of love, and of a sound mind" (II Timothy 1:7).** The Greek translation for the word sound in this scripture is sober, thinking sensibly, discipline, and or self-control. We must become accustomed to thinking with a mind controlled by the spirit of God. We must discipline our thoughts, and reject thoughts that are rooted in fear. An example of a fear-based thought is worrying about something that might happen. God says He has given us power, love, and a sound mind. This scripture shows us that fear is not from God. If we are constantly worried or afraid, we need to seek God for His peace. The word of God gives us these instructions and promises, **"Be careful for nothing; but in everything by prayer and supplication with thanksgiving let your requests be made known unto God. And the peace of God, which passeth all understanding, shall keep your hearts and minds through Christ Jesus" (Philippians 4: 6-7).**

We are told not to worry, but to pray about everything. We should make our requests known to God, and be thankful for all He has done. If we do these things, we are promised peace that will keep our hearts and minds. If we will pray, and keep our mind on His word, He will give us peace in every situation. The devil uses many forms of deception to keep souls bound. As has been stated, some are lead astray by false doctrine, but satan also binds souls with fear and intimidation. Jesus tells us that whatever we bind on earth will be bound in heaven; and whatever is loosed on earth is loosed in heaven (See Matthew 18:18). We have the power to bind what is evil, and loose what is good. We have even been given the power to loose fear into the enemy's camp.

The Bible says the fear of the Lord is the beginning of Wisdom (see Proverbs 9:10). Webster's Concise Dictionary defines one who is wise as having the ability to discern, and judge soundly between what is true and false. The Apostle Paul exhorted Timothy to instruct those who oppose truth patiently, with the hope that they will recover their minds from the snare of the devil (see II Timothy 2:26). The word snare in this scripture means, a noose, and a notch, a trick or temptation. Those deceived by false doctrine or bound by a spirit of fear are unable to discern between what is true and false. Putting our faith in God and His laws will make us wise. Faith in God will pull down the strongholds of fear and deception in our minds.

Strongholds are the way we think or view things. These are most often unproductive, unhealthy, and lead to sin. Strongholds are not only harmful to us, but they harm our children as well. We unknowingly pass our way of thinking down to our children. Often, we have inherited the way we think from our parents. When we are born again, we receive a new lineage through adoption by the spirit of God. The Bible says in Romans 8:15, **"For ye have not received the spirit of bondage again to fear; but ye have received the Spirit of adoption, whereby we cry, Abba, Father."** When we continue to allow our thoughts to be controlled by the mindset of the world, we are in bondage to fear. We should be controlling our thoughts; our thoughts should not be controlling us.

The Bible tells us to gird our minds, controlling what we allow to enter and dwell in them. Our thoughts should be centered on the hope of Jesus Christ. I Peter 1:13-16 says, **"Therefore, get your minds ready for work, keep yourselves under control, and fix your hopes fully on the gift you will receive when Yeshua the Messiah is revealed. As people who obey God, do not let yourselves be shaped by evil desires you used to have when you were still ignorant. On the contrary, following the Holy One who called you, become holy yourselves in your entire way of life; since the**

Tanakh says, "You are to be holy because I am holy" (JNT). We must have our minds in working order, and be prepared to deal with the circumstances that come our way. Our thoughts should be holy if we are to be holy, since holiness begins in the mind and the heart.

Also, we must stop dwelling on past sin or mistakes. Many are trapped in cycle of reliving their past in their present life, and in relationships with others. Past offences will cause us to fall if we allow them to. An unwillingness to change our view of these things, and put them in the past, prevents us from moving forward. We must let go, and let God be God in our lives. When we let go, and trust Him to be in control, He is able to do His sovereign work in our lives. This is not always easy, and it is a process that is different for everyone. It helps to remember that when we are living according to God's word; He will work with us in everything we do. We can't have the future God wants us to have when we don't let go of the past.

Lot and his family had been instructed not to look back when they fled the evil cities of Sodom and Gomorrah, but Lot's wife was disobedient. As a result, Lot's wife was turned into a pillar of salt (Genesis 19:17, 26). She must have been looking back at what she left behind instead of looking ahead towards her deliverance. If we are to be free, we must stop looking back towards our past transgressions, and the transgressions of others.

Jesus taught many times on the importance of forgiveness. If it weren't for God's willingness to forgive us, we could not be saved. All ties to the past must be broken by forgiveness. God does not want us bound to our past; that was one of His purposes for coming to this earth. He has a plan and a purpose for us. When we begin living for God, there may be things from our past we have to live with or overcome. Remember that God's word has a solution for every problem and circumstance. Some situations can't be changed, but He will help us manage them. Since God has given us our mind, He is the one that we should go to for help with our spiritual problems. He knows our mind better than any one else does. King David prayed **"Create in me a clean heart, O God; and renew a right spirit within me" (Psalm 51:10).** He knows when we want to change, and He will give us the power to do so.

Jesus said in Acts 1:8, **"But ye shall receive power, after that the Holy Ghost is come upon you: and ye shall be witnesses unto me both in Jerusalem, and in all Judea, and in Samara, and unto the uttermost part of the earth."** Jesus not only gives us power to become His witnesses, He empowers us to overcome as He overcame. We can overcome; we don't have to be victims, and we can control our thoughts and actions. John 16:33 says, **"These things I have spoken unto you, that in me ye might have peace. In the world ye shall have tribulation: but be of good cheer; I have overcome the world."**

Although there will be tribulation in this life, we are given power to overcome. We receive this power through a willingness to receive Jesus according to His word. John 1:12 says, **"But as many as received him, to them gave he power to become the sons of God, even to them that believe on his name."**

The word son in this scripture not only means son, but also daughter or child. The Bible tells us about those who overcame by the blood of the lamb, and the word of their testimony:

And the great dragon was cast out, that old serpent, called the Devil, and Satan, which deceiveth the whole world: he was cast out into the earth, and his angels were cast out with him. And I heard a loud voice saying in heaven, Now is come salvation, and strength, and the kingdom of our God, and the power of his Christ: for the accuser of our brethren is cast down, which accused them before our God day and night. And they overcame him by blood of the Lamb, and the word of their testimony; they loved not their lives unto the death (Revelation 12:9-11).

We need the blood of the lamb and the word of our testimony to overcome. We also must be willing to die to our life of sin and put God first. We cannot shrink back from our calling when tribulation comes. Those who lose their lives will keep them, and those who try to keep their lives will lose them (see Luke 9:24). When we overcome the trials and tribulations of this world, we will have a testimony. Jesus is the lamb slain from the foundation of the world. John the Baptist said of Jesus in John 1:36, **"And looking upon Jesus as he walked, he saith, Behold the Lamb of God!"** In order to have the blood of the lamb applied to our lives, we must be baptized in the name of Jesus. The Bible tells us that the promise of the Holy Ghost, and baptism in Jesus name is for everyone. Acts 2:39 says, **"For the promise is unto you, and to your children, and to all that are afar off, even as many as the Lord our God shall call."**

The promise is for us. Deliverance is for us. The Holy Ghost is for us. Where the spirit of the Lord is there is liberty and freedom. Jesus can deliver anyone from depression. He can deliver anyone from addiction to drugs, alcohol, and every other imaginable sin. He can heal wounds caused by abuse, and deliver us from the painful memories of the past. Jesus came to bind up the broken hearted, to proclaim liberty to the captives, and to open the prison doors for them who are bound. When we allow Jesus into our hearts, lives, and minds, we will receive power to overcome obstacles that we never thought we could. We can be changed, as the Bible says, from glory to glory. We can use what satan meant for our destruction against him. Jesus can turn our past into a weapon in our hands. He will use us to pierce the darkness, and with the word of our testimony we can set others free.

The Call

In weariness, oppression, sickness or depression;

Come to me child, you are my possession.

I am your strength in every situation,

Your way out of every frustration.

I give guidance at your request,

An answer for every problem do I possess.

Listen to my voice, my words are true.

On your decision I wait, the choice is up to you.

I have given man this decision to make.

A way of salvation or destruction to take.

It is my desire and will for all,

Every soul I created has a specific call.

In vain I do nothing, no false move do I make;

A purpose, a pathway, a road of escape.

So flee from deception, I call you this day.

With open arms I receive you, In my word I do say.

I give hope for tomorrow, I give it to all,

Those who are willing to respond to my call.

Chapter Two

The Garment of Praise for the Spirit of Heaviness

I can testify that Jesus is a deliverer because He delivered me. For many years I suffered with depression. Depression is one of the most debilitating conditions that people are oppressed with. When someone has a physical ailment they can go to a doctor for treatment. Usually in time they will recover. When someone visits a doctor for depression, they are given a drug so they can cope with how they feel. The psychoactive drugs prescribed only mask the symptoms. Although the medical field can't cure someone of depression, the good news is, Jesus can. I lived for 38 years without knowing the truth of the gospel. I never knew about deliverance. I knew Jesus died for us, but I never knew He could deliver us from addictions or depression. This is the message that I want to convey in the following chapters of this book.

Like many people, I knew about Jesus, but never understood who He really is. I was taught to believe in God, but never knew Him until he became real to me on December 19, 2000. That was the day I received the baptism of the Holy Ghost with the evidence of speaking with other tongues. Two days later I received a call, and was told my niece had two brain tumors. One was tangerine sized, and was blocking the spinal fluid from circulating normally in her brain. The other was sausage sized, and involved the nerves in her neck. The doctors said she required immediate surgery, and that the surgery could be fatal or leave her a cripple.

I was at home when I heard the news, and I ran into the bathroom crying. I began to speak in tongues. That time seemed different than what I had experienced at Church. A voice told me, which I knew was God's, "don't worry, the little girl won't die." Immediately I felt at peace. My niece is healed of cancer today. She was completely healed by the Great Physician. The doctors had their reports, but God had one of His own. She came through the surgery, and has had no reoccurrence since. She is a normal little girl today. It's always best to listen to the report of the Lord.

Many things have come down the road of my life since that day. Through them all, I have learned that Jesus has the answer for everything we are going through. Even when we must simply wait on Him, He will give us peace in every situation. I am thankful for all that Jesus has done, is doing, and will do. I am also thankful for the people who prayed for my niece, and for my Pastor. He fasted two days for my niece's healing, and took the time to come to the hospital to pray. God is still raising up great men who are not afraid to speak the truth of the Gospel, and move in the gifts of the spirit with integrity.

As I said, for years I suffered with depression. There were many factors in my life that brought me to the place where I finally sought help from a psychiatrist. I can't name a specific one. However, I can speak of a name that delivered me. I can testify of a name that brought healing to my soul and spirit. That is the name of Jesus. Jesus is a name above all names. All the power of God is in the name of Jesus. Jesus is the only answer when it comes to disturbances of the mind.

These are some of the promises foretold in Isaiah 61:1-3: Good tidings will be preached to the meek. The broken-hearted will have their wounds bound up, and liberty will be proclaimed to the captives. The prison doors will be opened for those who are bound, and those who mourn will be comforted. Beauty will be exchanged for ashes, and the oil of joy will be exchanged for mourning. Also, a garment of praise will be exchanged for the spirit of heaviness.

The word meek, used in Isaiah 61:1, when translated to Hebrew is depressed in mind or circumstances. We have all had things happen to us that have made us discouraged. We have all been hurt and broken-hearted. The good news is that we have a God that will comfort us. The Hebrew translation for the word heaviness, used in Isaiah 61:3 is feeble, obscure, somewhat dark, darkish, and wax dim. These words accurately describe the condition of our mind when the spirit of heaviness is oppressing us. This portion of scripture proclaims deliverance and healing from the damaging experiences that everyone will face in this life. According to scripture, depression is a spirit.

Physical illness and suffering can cause an individual to become negative and discouraged. However, depression is a way of thinking that takes root in the mind or soul. Depression is a spiritual problem, not a physical problem. We must make every effort not to be overcome with negative thoughts. Jesus is our example, and He is our only way of solving spiritual problems. The word Christian means Christ like. If we are to be called Christians, we must make every effort to be like Him. Jesus would not take a mind-altering drug when it was offered to Him on the cross.

Mark 15:23 says, **"And they gave him to drink wine mingled with Myrrh: but he received it not."** The Greek translation of the word Myrrh is to tincture, embitter or a narcotic. Webster's Dictionary defines the word tincture as a solution of a medicinal substance in an alcoholic menstruum. Webster's defines the word menstruum as a substance that dissolves a solid or holds it in suspension. Easton's Bible Dictionary says, "It was a custom of the Jews to give those who were condemned to death by crucifixion "wine mingled with myrrh" to produce insensibility". Every one of us will go through trials and tribulation:

Emotional suffering is inevitable in this life. But it has meaning—a purpose. Suffering is a signal that life matters. Specifically, it is usually a signal that something in our lives that matters a great deal needs to be addressed. Depression, guilt, anxiety, shame, chronic anger, emotional numbing—all of these reactions signal that something is amiss and requires special attention. The depth of suffering is a sign of the soul's desire for a better, more creative, more principled life. When faced with a patient in deep depression, should we immediately focus on relief of the pain? On the contrary, we should respond by saying that the pain is a signal of the intensity of the person's spirit: "The strength and intensity of your suffering indicates the strength and intensity of your spirit. Your discomfort shows how alive you are. Now imagine if you could learn to turn all that self-destructive energy into creative energy and a love of life." The degree to which we suffer indicates the degree to which we are alive. When we take drugs to ease our suffering, we stifle our psychological and spiritual life. (Breggin and Cohen 3)

Trials that are handled in the correct manner will bring victory to our lives and make us overcomers. The crucifixion of Jesus brought about a resurrection, and victory over death for all of mankind. When we cover up our problems with drugs instead of dealing with them, we can't live victorious lives. The Apostle Paul said, **"For I reckon that the sufferings of this present time are not worthy to be compared with the glory which shall be revealed in us" (Romans 8:18)**. Although we can't literally compare the suffering we go through to the horrible death Jesus died, there is analogy in a spiritual sense. Paul told the Church, I die daily (see I Corinthians 15:31). When we read the scriptures we learn that Paul struggled with his fleshly desires and sin. He went through much persecution and suffering, but he believed in the delivering power of God to bring him though his circumstances.

Galatians 2:20 says, **"I am crucified with Christ: nevertheless I live; yet not I, but Christ liveth in me: and the life which I now live in the flesh I live by the faith of the Son of God, who loved me, and gave himself for me."** Paul wasn't saying that he died in a literal sense. He meant that he died to his flesh and carnal mind. Jesus conquered sin, death, and the grave for us. He has walked before us in everything we go through. He has compassion on us because He suffered infirmity like us (see Hebrews 5:2). Jesus overcame His suffering, and He will enable us to overcome our suffering. If we trust in Him, he will strengthen us. He will be the Lily of our darkest valley and our Bright and Morning Star. He is the Author and Finisher of our faith.

I Peter 4:12-13 says, **"Beloved, think it not strange concerning the fiery trial which is to try you, as though some strange thing happened unto you: But rejoice, inasmuch as ye are partakers of Christ's sufferings; that, when his glory shall be revealed, ye may be glad also with exceeding joy."** When we die to our way of handling situations, following Christ's example, we bring the power of God into our lives. Christians are supposed to take up their own cross and follow Jesus (See Mark 10:21). Are we following Him if we are turning to mind-altering drugs? Should we go to a psychiatrist for drugs because we can't deal with the problems in our life? Jesus refused the drug, and He prayed. To be like Him, we must follow His example.

Bipolar mood disorder is a label given for what was once called manic depression. There are many different labels given by modern psychiatry today. When a person receives a label they believe they are ill, and that something is wrong with them that requires medication. Once this diagnosis is given, some may believe they are disabled and that they can't change:

They may feel overwhelmed and no longer in charge of themselves or their lives. Too often, all this is made worse when people seek help from a psychiatrist. First, they receive a medical-sounding diagnosis. Often they are told that they have "panic attacks" or "obsessive-compulsive disorder" or "major depression" or "manic-depressive (bipolar) disorder." Immediately, this confirms their feelings of helplessness. Psychiatric diagnosis, a system of thought that is alien to an individual's everyday sense of themselves, is imposed from the outside. Being diagnosed implies that the problem is a disorder or even a brain disease inside them, yet totally beyond their control. (Breggin and Cohen 92)

This is debilitating and alters the course of normal everyday life. Some may not work, and many end up on social security disability. They believe they have an excuse to remain the way they are. When a person has no schedule to follow or purpose to their life, their idle mind becomes the devil's workshop. Their thoughts become progressively negative because they have no hope, dreams, or ambitions. When a psychiatrist diagnosed me with bipolar mood disorder after talking to me for about half an hour, I accepted the diagnosis. I thought drugs would cure me of my depression, but that wasn't the case. I had never addressed the problems in my life or searched for the reason behind the way I felt. I never knew I could change the way I felt by changing my attitude and outlook on life. My attitude was one of my worst problems. I have come to realize that drugs can't change attitudes. Also, while under the care of the psychiatrist, I was given an increased dosage of drugs whenever I told him I didn't feel any better. He also increased the dosage to control my "racing thoughts." Initially, I was prescribed 50 mg of the drug Zoloft for depression. Before long I was taking 100 mg. Prior to my hospitalization, I was on a higher dose than that.

I began to feel nervous and paranoid. I told the psychiatrist, and the psychiatrist diagnosed the nervousness as a panic attack. He prescribed Valium, and told me to take a pill whenever I had a panic attack. I was soon taking approximately 40 mg of Valium a day. In the end, I was hospitalized for addiction to Valium. During my stay in the hospital, the psychiatrist prescribed Tegretol to replace the Valium. After my release from the hospital, I was taking 300 mg of Tegretol and 100 mg of Zoloft. These drugs caused my vision to be blurred, and I felt disoriented. When I told the psychiatrist, he told me that those were normal side effects of the drug, and that I would get used to them. Studies have shown that these drugs have dangerous side effects that can lead to permanent damage and even death:

Psychiatric drugs in general produce varying degrees of toxic psychoses and other severe mental abnormalities, including anxiety, depression, and mania. Confirming the frequency of adverse reactions to psychiatric drugs, a German study found that 11 percent of hospitalized psychiatric patients developed adverse drug-symptoms that were severe enough to warrant discontinuation. The researchers observed that life-threatening reactions were relatively common, occurring in 1.8 percent of the patients. By far the most severe reaction was "toxic delirium," a drug-induced state of confusion, disorientation, and generalized mental impairment. Elderly patients are especially prone to toxic psychoses as well as to less intense mental impairments from almost any mind-altering drug. Typical effects on the elderly include stimulation, excitement, insomnia, depression, and memory problems. Toxic psychoses, which occur in varying degrees of severity, are also diagnosed as delirium, organic brain syndrome, confusion, or mania. Sometimes a doctor, family member, or patient may notice one or two possible symptoms of toxic psychoses—such as agitation, disorientation, incoherence, disturbed concentration, memory difficulties, or hallucinations—without recognizing the severity of the overall mental dysfunction. Anxiety and depression are frequently caused by psychiatric drugs. They can appear in either the presence or absence of toxic psychoses. (Breggin and Cohen 61)

Another danger involved in taking psychoactive drugs is drug-induced mania:

Drug-induced mania is a severe psychotic disorder whose symptoms include extreme overactivity, insomnia, racing thoughts, frantic and exhausting outbursts of energy, grandiosity and fantasies of omnipotence that may lead to bizarre and destructive actions, paranoia, and sometimes even suicide.

People undergoing drug-induced mania have been known to throw away their life's savings on unrealistic schemes or to ruin or quit jobs and marriages that were previously successful. Some end up in mental hospitals or jails. Others commit violence. If we accept the estimate that approximately 1 percent of depressed patients treated with Prozac will develop potentially devastating manic reactions, that works out to be a thousand people out of every million. These figures are disastrous in themselves, but in routine clinical practice the reactions would be much more frequent and severe. Also, a worsening of depression was listed in Prozac's official label as a commonly reported possible adverse effect of Prozac until it was edited out on the very last day or two. Who edited it out? The FDA itself. What was the explanation? The agency wanted to shorten the distracting "laundry list" of adverse reactions indicated by the drug company. Yet depression as a common result of taking antidepressants surely warrants emphasis rather than complete deletion from the drug label. Because of the deletion, the profession and the public remain unaware of the frequent reports by Eli Lily's own investigators that Prozac can worsen depression. (Breggin and Cohen 108)

According to Breggin and Cohen, the drug Prozac puts children at a great risk for drug induced mania:

Prozac even more commonly induces mania in children. In a study intended to tout the drugs safety and efficacy, 6 percent of the children were forced to drop out due to Prozac-induced mania. A similar drug, Luvox, produced a 4 percent rate of "manic reactions" in children, according to the Physician's Desk Reference. Luvox was being taken by Eric Harris at the time he committed the murders at Columbine High School in Littleton, Colorado, on April 20, 1999. Without a doubt, Prozac and other antidepressants are causing tens of thousands of psychotic reactions that can ruin the lives not only of the afflicted individuals, but also of their family members (61-62).

I myself can testify that drugs did not make my life better, they only made things worse. They made me feel worse about myself, and did not help me handle the issues we all must manage in every day life. In fact, instead of helping me feel better about my situation so I could bring order to my life, drugs brought shame and disorder. While I was hospitalized, the psychiatrist set up a family meeting with everyone sitting in a circle. They talked about me like I wasn't there. He took one member of my family aside to discuss something. I was never told what it was, but the experience was dehumanizing:

What happens when we start viewing a human being as an object? We lose our capacity for rationality and for love. It is impossible to reduce a person's emotional suffering to biochemical aberrations without doing something psychologically and morally destructive to that person. We reduce the reality of that individual's life to a narrowly focused speculation about brain chemistry. In taking such a distorted view of the person, doctors do harm to themselves. They suppress their natural tendency to be empathic toward other human beings. Thus, in their efforts to be "objective" and "scientific", biological psychiatrists and doctors end up doing very destructive things to people, including themselves. (Breggin and Cohen 10)

All human beings need to know that they are loved and have someone they can turn to who cares about them. When we have no one else to turn to, we can turn to Jesus. One of the things I love most about Jesus is that we can trust Him. He won't talk about our problems with anyone else, and we can trust Him with all our secrets. When He deals with certain things in our lives, He doesn't discuss them with anyone else. This is why we should take our personal problems to Him. It's not that we shouldn't trust anyone, and it is good to be accountable to the right people. However, no human has the power to deliver us from spiritual problems. Our friends can't be there for us all the time, and they can't deliver us from depression. Jesus is the only one who has the power to deliver our soul. Medication can't solve our problems anymore than drinking alcohol can:

Taking psychiatric drugs can make it very hard to know what you are really feeling. You may feel better at first while taking an antidepressant, stimulant, or tranquilizer; but now you wonder if the improvement was due to your own personal efforts at improving your life or perhaps to changes in your circumstances or even the passage of time. Psychiatric drugs blunt and confuse these essential emotional signals. Our emotions depend on our brain function, and the brain is an intricate, delicate organ that can easily be thrown out of whack by drugs. Sometimes drugs give us "false positive" signals, such as an artificial high or euphoria. When euphoric, we may remain stuck in unsatisfactory, frustrating situations or take unrealistic or even grandiose risks. There are no drugs that can improve mental function, self-understanding, or human relations. Any drug that effects mental processes does so by impairing them. (Breggin and Cohen 95, 98)

However, there are actions that we can take that will help us to overcome depression. Of course we need a relationship with God, but we also need a willingness to change our thinking. Instead of focusing on our own problems, we must learn to think about the needs of others. This is the example Jesus gave us. He always looked to the needs of others. No where in scripture did He focus on His problems, or feel sorry for Himself. Also, we must allow the power of the Holy Ghost to work in our lives. This can be accomplished by developing a lifestyle of prayer and fasting. Prayer and fasting will help us overcome sin, which is a root cause of depression. Prayer and fasting increases faith, and faith weakens the devil. When we pray and fast, we are focusing on God instead of our problems. This will enable us to see everything in a different light. He will increase in our lives as we decrease. Fasting and prayer not only subdues our flesh, but also weakens the devil.

King David said in Psalm 35:13, **"I humbled my soul with fasting."** The meaning of the word humbled in Hebrew is submit-self. James 4:7 says, **"Submit yourselves therefore to God. Resist the devil, and he will flee from you."** Fasting is a tool given to us by God to have victory over our enemies and our own fleshly nature. When the disciples asked Jesus why they couldn't cast out a demon out, Jesus told them it was because of their unbelief. He also said, **"Howbeit this kind goeth not out but by prayer and fasting" (Matthew 17:21)**. Our own carnal desires are our worst enemies. The Bible says in I John 2:16, **"For all that is in the world, the lust of the flesh, and the lust of the eyes, and the pride of life, is not of the Father, but is of the world."**

Prayer and fasting are the most effective ways to overcome the sinful works of our flesh. Galatians 5:19-21 gives us a list of the works of the flesh. **"Now the works of the flesh are manifest, which are these; Adultery, fornication, uncleanness, lasciviousness, Idolatry, witchcraft, hatred, variance, emulations, wrath, strife, seditions, heresies, Envyings, murders, drunkenness, revellings, and such like: of the which I tell you before, as I have also told you in time past, that they which do such things shall not inherit the kingdom of God."** The Bible tells us that those that belong to Christ will crucify the flesh and its lusts. Fasting will help us to accomplish this. God's people have always practiced fasting in both the Old and New Testament. To learn how Queen Ester obtained favor with God through prayer and fasting, which resulted in the salvation of her people, read the book of Ester.

Isaiah 58:6 tells us that fasting will loose the bands of wickedness, undo the heavy burden, let the oppressed go free, and break every yoke. A yoke was used to control animals. The devil attempts to put yokes on us to control us. Fasting will weaken the devil, and his influence in our lives because fasting increases our faith. Fasting will help us to see things differently, and we will be able to overcome. I have fasted because I had a bad attitude, and I can tell you it works. Fasting benefits not only our spirit and soul, but also is good for our bodies because fasting removes toxins. Fasting also helps us to cultivate the fruit of the spirit, one of these being temperance (see Galatians 5:22-23). Temperance means to have control or balance. This helps us physically because we will be able to control what, and how much we eat. If we cultivate temperance, we will be able to maintain our proper weight. It is less expensive than Jenny Craig or Weight Watchers.

I am thankful for fasting. It is not always easy, but it has helped me to gain control over my life. It is important that we follow God's word in every aspect of our lives. This includes our body as well as our soul and spirit. We can easily be deceived into believing we need diet pills, and special programs for weight control. These methods are costly, and don't offer a permanent solution to weight problems. If we are willing to discipline ourselves, we will have lasting results.

This is true in every area of our lives. We don't have to be limited by what this world has to offer. There is no limit to what God can do in our lives if we allow Him to. We don't have to be labeled by this world. I will never forget when I heard Gayla Foster give the message on labels and their damaging effects. I had never heard anyone speak on that subject before. Later I told her that I believed and appreciated what she said. I had experienced it, and I knew what she said was true. I told her what I had experienced, and how Jesus delivered me. When she spoke the next day, she asked me to give my testimony. I saw her afterwards, and I told her that she should write a book because it would help a lot of people. She told me that I should write a book. After she said that, a memory came back to me.

In 1989 I was attending college to earn a bachelors degree in education. In one class I took, we were given the assignment of writing a letter addressed to ourselves stating what we would accomplish in ten years. The instructor said she would mail the letter to us in ten years. I had a lot of big dreams; one of them was to write a book. Ten years later when I received the letter in the mail, my life was a mess. I hadn't accomplished any of the things I had planned to. Busting out in tears, I tore the letter into little pieces. Writing a book was one of the things I had wanted to accomplish, and thought I never could. Now I have been given another chance.

Jesus is so good to us; He has a way of turning things around. He can take our mistakes, and turn them into something useful. He can bring life into a dead situation. I made up my mind to write a book in to help others who feel their situations are hopeless. At that time Jesus gave me this word concerning depression: "Depression is not a sickness or disease. It is a state of mind that can only be remedied by the will and desire of an individual to change their way of thinking." When we make up our mind to change the way we think, we are on our way to deliverance.

The word depression is not found in the Bible. The Bible calls depression the spirit of heaviness. As has been previously stated, Isaiah 61:3 says that God will give us a garment of praise for the spirit of heaviness. It is the will of God to deliver us from the spirit of heaviness. King Solomon, the wisest king that ever lived, wrote this proverb. **"Heaviness in the heart of man maketh it stoop: but a good word maketh it glad" (Proverbs 12:25).** The Hebrew translation of the word heaviness in this scripture is anxiety, fear, and sorrow. The word heart implies the will or intellect, and the word stoop implies to depress or prostrate.

The power of life and death is in the tongue. Our words have the ability to lift us up or tear us down. Our thinking is largely responsible for what we say. We must be willing to exchange our negative thoughts for positive ones, and the word of God will help us do this. When our thoughts are negative, satan has been given authority in our soul. Jesus has made it possible for us to overcome satan's negative influence on our soul. We have been given power to overcome the oppression of the adversary.

The words spoken by the prophet Isaiah were fulfilled when God was manifested in the flesh, and the earthly ministry of Jesus was carried out. The Bible tells us that Jesus read the words of the prophet Isaiah in the synagogue. **"The spirit of the Lord is upon me, because he hath anointed me to preach the gospel to the poor; he hath sent me to heal the brokenhearted, to preach deliverance to the captives, and recovering of sight to the blind, to set at liberty them that are bruised, To preach the acceptable year of the Lord.**

And he began to say unto them, This day is this scripture fulfilled in your ears" (Luke 4:18-19, 21).

When this scripture was inspired, the Jewish people observed a holiday called the Year of Jubilee. This was a year when the land was restored to the poor. This was a type of redemption and restoration. Some Bible scholars believe Jesus was making an analogy to this holiday when He spoke of the acceptable year of the Lord. It is interesting to note that the word bruised used in this scripture means to crush, and the word oppression used to describe the affliction of the people in II Kings 13:4 has a similar meaning. It also means to crush, distress, afflict, and force. Isn't that what the enemy has done to us?

The sin of the people caused Israel to be oppressed by the king of Syria. The Bible says that Jehoahaz sought the Lord. God listened because He saw their oppression, and sent Israel a savior. He set them at liberty because of an intercessor (see II Kings 13:1-5). Jesus is our intercessor. When we have been crushed by the effects of sin, and seek Him with all our heart, He will set us free from oppression. This includes oppression from the spirit of depression

The effects of this spirit on our lives can result in a feeling of hopelessness, loss of interest in life, and spiritual darkness. The anger and fear that accompanies depression causes our thoughts to become negative. Negative thoughts result in deception because they directly oppose the word of God. We become deceived into believing that we have to carry our burden alone and there is no hope. What we need to do is give the weight on our shoulders to Jesus.

Jesus says, **"For my yoke is easy, and my burden is light" (Matthew 11:30).** Jesus wants to us to give Him our problems. The Bible tells to cast our cares on Him because He cares for us. He is able to deliver us from depression, and anoint us with a garment of praise. The word praise in Isaiah 61:3 means hymn. We will wear a song of praise when He lifts the burden off of us. We will wake up in the morning knowing we have hope, and we will have a song in our hearts. Isaiah 10:27 says, **"And it shall come to pass in that day, that his burden shall be taken away from off thy shoulder, and his yoke from off thy neck, and the yoke shall be destroyed because of the anointing."** Jesus, the anointed one, will lift the burden. He will destroy the yoke that the enemy has used to control us.

Understanding that depression is a spirit enlightens us to the fact that taking drugs that alter our mind will not help us overcome. I agree with Gayla Foster's statement, "You can't fight spiritual warfare with chemical warfare." When a person is depressed they aren't sick, and they don't need a doctor's treatment. When a person is oppressed by depression they need deliverance. There is only one deliverer, and His name is Jesus.

Most doctors prescribe drugs for depression, and the drugs are sometimes accompanied by counseling. Most therapists believe we need to go back to our past, but scripture doesn't tell us to look to the past. Scripture tells us to forget the former things. Old things are passed away, and all things are become new. Sometimes we focus on past or present problems, instead of obeying the word of God and focusing on Him. We mustn't let our problems become our gods. It is possible to let our past, and our problems take the place of God in our lives. We mustn't let our problems become a golden calf.

A majority of spiritual problems have their root cause in sin. I feel I can make this statement because I was in bondage to sin that manifested itself as mental illness. My depression was a result of the effects of sin on my life. When the sin problem was dealt with, the mental illness went away. Another disorder that has become prevalent in society is obsessive compulsive disorder. An individual that repeats the same action over again until it causes a disturbance in their life will be labeled with OCD (obsessive compulsive disorder).

OCD has its root cause in fear, preoccupation with self, and undisciplined thought processes. This statement is not popular, but it is true. I have learned it is easy to become bound by these things when life's circumstances come our way. The Holy Ghost can set anyone free from the spiritual bondage that leads to OCD. We must do our part by letting certain things go. There have been times when I have gone back to check my car door or the door to my house to be sure I locked it. If I went back to check these things all day long, it would cause problems in my daily routine. We can't allow fear and deceitful thoughts to control our minds. It's when these influences are given reign in our mind that normal functioning is impaired. We must learn to manage our thinking.

It's not uncommon to struggle with fear and unbelief. However, we must choose to believe God's word. Scripture teaches us that unbelief is sin. Let's look at a few examples in scripture. **"Take heed, brethren, lest there be in any of you an evil heart of unbelief, in departing from the living God" (Hebrews 3:12).** Revelation 21:8 says the fearful and unbelieving will have their place in the lake of fire, along with murderers, liars, and the abominable. In I Peter 2:6-8, we are told that Jesus is the chief cornerstone, and whoever believes in Him will not be confounded. Believing in Jesus must be more than a statement because the word of God says even demons believe and tremble (see James 2:19).

Therefore, it involves a total belief in the word of God that leads to obedience. Obedience will give us victory over the sin that confounds us. The word confounded means to disgrace, dishonor or to make ashamed. Unbelief and fear are the underlying cause of jealousy, anger, depression, and lead to sin that results in shame. Romans 14:23 tells us that whatsoever is not of faith is sin, and the Bible also tells us that unbelief is disobedience.

When we really believe what the word says, we will think differently. We will believe that Jesus has the power to deliver us, and His promises are true. Depression sets in when we become focused on ourselves, instead of focusing on the God who has the power to solve the problem. Again, overcoming depression requires effort on our part because depression takes hold in the thought realm. How we choose to think can be either a blessing or a curse to us.

Positive thinking will cause blessing in our lives, and negative thinking will curse us. What we believe and say will come to pass in our lives. As a man believes in his heart, so is he. There is great power in speaking positively. We should always make positive statements, even when we don't feel positive. When we make a habit of speaking positively instead of negatively, we will see our circumstances change. Speak the word of God, and believe His promises. The Bible says that God cannot lie, but Jeremiah 17:9 says our hearts are deceitful and desperately wicked. Therefore, we can't base what we believe on our emotions.

The reader should be informed of the fact that there are no laboratory findings to substantiate the existence of depressive mood disorders. The criteria used to make these diagnoses are based on man's theory. I have cited portions of the American Psychiatric Associations diagnostic criteria for bipolar I disorder in order to give the reader an idea of how a diagnosis is reached:

A. Presence (or history) of one or more major depressive episodes (397). Some of the criteria listed for a major depressive episode are: depressed mood most of the day, diminished interest in activities, significant weight loss, decrease in appetite, insomnia or hyperinsomia, psychomotor agitation, fatigue, indecisiveness, inappropriate guilt, feelings of worthlessness, recurrent thoughts of death (356).

B. Presence (or history) of at least one hypomanic episode (397). The criteria for diagnosing a hypomanic episode includes a distinct period of elevated, expansive, or irritable mood lasting at least four days. Three or more of the following symptoms must be present: Inflated self-esteem, decreased need for sleep, more talkative than usual. Also including, flight ideas, racing thoughts, distractibility, increase in goal directed activities, excessive involvement in pleasurable activities that have a high potential for painful consequences (e.g. the person engages in unrestrained buying sprees, sexual indiscretions, or foolish business investments). The episode is not severe enough to cause hospitalization. These symptoms are not due to the effects of medication or drug abuse (368).

C. There has never been a manic or mixed episode (397). The criteria for manic or mixed episodes are similar to a major depressive episode. The main difference between the three is the duration of time that the symptoms are present. However, in a mixed episode the criteria for a manic and a major depressive episode are both met.

D. The mood symptoms in criteria A and B are not better accounted for by Schizoaffective Disorder and are not superimposed on Schizophrenia, Schizophreniform Disorder, Delusional Disorder, or Psychotic Disorder.

E. The symptoms cause clinically significant distress or impairment in social, occupational, or other important areas of functioning (397).

It should be noted that according to the American Psychiatric Association, there is a familiar pattern present in these disorders. This is stated in the DSM-IV-TR regarding Major Depressive Disorders:

Major Depressive Disorder and BiPolar I and II Disorder appear to be more common among first-degree biological relatives of persons with Clyclothymic disorder than among the general population. There may also be an increased familiar risk of Substance-Related Disorders. In addition, Clycothymic Disorder may be more common in the first degree-biological relatives of individuals with BiPolar Mood I Disorder (399).

Cyclothymic Disorder is most simply defined as chronic, fluctuating, mood disturbances. Before I was born again, I experienced mood disturbances, racing thoughts, and many of the symptoms listed above (some of these may have been drug-induced). Medication did not solve these problems because their root cause was sin and an undisciplined lifestyle. We really do have the power to control our thoughts and behavior. The Bible teaches us that the iniquity of the fathers will be passed to the children to the third, and fourth generation of those who hate Him (See Exodus 20:5).

Jesus said, **"If ye love me, keep my commandments" (John 14:15).** According to God, we hate Him when we don't live by His laws. When we read the above symptoms, we must admit that many are sin and a lack of self-discipline. Although some of the circumstances in our lives aren't our fault, we must learn to rise above the circumstances that lead to depression.

Depression is often brought on by a series of traumatic events. Rebellion, bitterness, and shame resulting from abuse or rejection in childhood are an open door for depression. In general, unforgiveness of any kind leads to depression and other sin. Unforgiveness negatively effects the way we think and act. It also effects the way we feel about others and life in general. Unforgiveness directed towards ourselves, known as shame, will cause us to act in a way that causes more shame. Shame then becomes a trap that the enemy uses to keep us bound. Freedom from shame requires daily prayer, a willingness to forgive ourself, and a willingness to allow God to take us through a healing process.

There are times when we have to deal with things that happened in the past, but this doesn't mean we dwell on the past. God will sometimes bring past incidents to our mind because we need to forgive so we can be healed and delivered. Many times there are wounds in our spirit that we don't realize are there. These must be healed so we can be made whole. We must be willing to allow God to reveal these hidden things to us. When we refuse to forgive ourselves, we are demonstrating a lack of faith in the power of God's love. Our greatest weapon against shame is to believe in God's love and forgiveness towards us.

The loss of a loved one can lead to depression. Sometimes people become angry with God because of the loss, and the end result is rebellion. While I was hospitalized for addiction to

Valium, I saw a woman who didn't communicate with anyone, and I asked what had happened to her. The nurse told me that a relative had died, and she became so depressed she attempted suicide. They performed shock therapy so she wouldn't remember what had happened. She just sat there with a blank look on her face. This is an example of how the world handles situations that should be given to God. We must remember we have hope. We are not alone, and the word of God has the answers we need. Losing someone we love is a very devastating thing to go through, and I'm not minimizing it. When tragedy strikes, we have a choice between two alternatives, the world's way or God's way. We need to take the loss of loved ones, and all other problems to the cross.

Another root cause of depression may be sin committed by someone else. When a child has been abused, the abuse causes a wound in their spirit. They become angry, depressed, and fearful. When the feelings caused by the abuse are not dealt with, a root of bitterness becomes planted in their heart. They grow into angry adults that have low self-esteem. These individuals have problems in their personal relationships. They often feel the need to control situations and other people. This is a result of the fear and helplessness they felt as a child. Abuse also causes its victims to suffer from feelings of rejection that result in shame. They feel somehow responsible for the act perpetrated on them, even though it wasn't their fault. They aren't capable of loving themselves, and this effects their ability to love others. Many times, they will end up abusing their children. Often, this self-hatred will lead to drug abuse and addiction. However, they don't have to remain victims. The perfect work performed at Calvary can change a victim of abuse into a victorious overcomer.

Psychoactive drugs will not help heal someone who is grieving, or has suffered a traumatic experience. What ever has happened to us, the Lord promises to deliver us. He promises us perfect peace if our mind is stayed on Him. **"Thou wilt keep him in perfect peace, whose mind is stayed on thee: because he trusteth in thee" (Isaiah 26:3).** When we allow our view on life, and our actions to be controlled by our emotions, we are in for a bumpy ride. Our emotions can change like the weather in the Midwest.

Taking medication to control our feelings, and alter our mind is against the word of God. Jesus died a horrible death for us to live in victory. We can live in victory because His word says so. What if the apostles were on antidepressants? Would they have accomplished all that they did? Let's face the fact that they had it a lot rougher that we do. The word of God is true, and we must put our faith and hope in it. Jesus took the shame of every human being upon himself. He took our place so we wouldn't have to pay the price for our sin. The Bible says the wages of sin are death, but He paid those wages for us. We need to be thankful. Sometimes we are unthankful, focusing only on ourselves. We need to focus on the One who is the answer to our problems. We need to pray a prayer of repentance if we begin to feel sorry for ourselves. If we look around, we can always find someone worse off than we are. We should be thankful for what the Lord has done for us.

The Bible warns us what can happen to those who are unthankful. Romans 1:21 says **"Because that, when they knew God, they glorified him not as God, neither were they thankful; but became vain in their imaginations, and their foolish heart was darkened."** The word vain used in this scripture refers to idolatry. Again, we must not let problems, and circumstances become our gods. Every day we should enter His courts with thanksgiving and praise. Romans 1: 24-32 tells us of the sin and perversion that will overtake those who are unthankful. Let's not allow ourselves to be overcome by these evil things. Let's choose the way of deliverance, and healing through the word of God.

We must run to Jesus, not to a psychiatrist when we are hurt or depressed. No human is able to put broken hearts or lives back together. Only Jesus can do that. He can even put broken families back together. I have seen it with my own eyes. We must think positively and look upward. Psalm 121 says:

I will lift up mine eyes unto the hills, from whence commeth my help. My help commeth from the Lord, which made heaven and earth. He will not suffer thy foot to be moved: he that keepeth thee will not slumber. Behold, he that keepeth Israel shall neither slumber nor sleep. The Lord is thy keeper: the Lord is thy shade upon thy right hand. The sun shall not smite thee by day, nor the moon by night. The Lord shall preserve thee from all evil: he shall preserve thy soul. The Lord shall preserve thy going out and thy coming in from this time forth, and even for evermore.

We need to lift up our eyes to the hills, and not look down to the things of this world. Our help comes from above, not below.

God's word promises us that He will be there for us, and protect us from harm.

When we feel cast down, we need to ask ourselves why we feel the way we do, and take our situation to the Lord in prayer. King David is our example because he took all his problems to God. The Bible says that David had many trials and human faults, but was still called a man after God's own heart. David encouraged himself in the Lord, and the Lord always delivered him.

David prayed in Psalm 43:5, **"Why art thou cast down, O my soul? and why are thou disquieted with in me? hope in God: for I shall yet praise him, who is the health of my countenance, and my God."** After asking himself, why are you cast down? He encouraged himself by saying, hope in God. He gave God praise, and thanksgiving in spite of his situation. Even though he felt cast down, he chose to think positively. The word health used in this scripture implies something that was saved: deliverance, aid, victory, help, salvation, and welfare.

David went to God believing He would deliver him out of his trial. David always looked to God for help; this is why he never stayed cast down for long in spite of his human frailties. David was able to overcome life's obstacles because he had a repentant heart, and he was a worshipper. He always worshiped God no matter what happened. God is seeking people who are worshipers, repentant, and have faith in Him. Worship is very important to God, and will enable us to defeat our adversary. Worship will bring us victory because when we worship, we bring God into our situation.

Repentance and forgiveness are needed if our worship is to be pure, and should be a part of our everyday life. Worship is evidence that we have faith that God will deliver us. The Bible tells us that God inhabits the praises of His people. When God comes into any situation, He can change it for the good. If we are not worshipping God, we will be worshipping something else. We need to follow David's example, and worship God regardless of how we feel. Even in the worst situation, if we are willing to worship, God will deliver us. The Bible tells us He always delivered David.

David was on the run, and living in Ziklag. He was running from King Saul who wanted to kill him. While David and his men were away, the Amalekites invaded the town. They burnt everything in the town, and took the women and children. The Bible says, **"And David was greatly distressed; for the people spake of stoning him, because the soul of all the people was grieved, every man for his sons and for his daughters: but David encouraged himself in the Lord his God" (I Samuel 30:6).**

The previous passage of scripture gives an example of what God's people should do when adversity comes. David's first response was to seek God. This resulted in David's deliverance out of trouble, and victory over his enemy. David took the women and children back, and also took spoil from the Amalekites. If God delivered David, restoring more to him than he had lost, He will do the same for us. God is no respecter of persons. The apostle Paul said in II Timothy 3:11, **"Persecutions, afflictions, which came unto me at Antioch,**

at Iconium, at Lystra; what persecutions I endured: but out of them all the Lord delivered me." God can deliver us just as He delivered Paul.

Psalm 91:5 says, **"Thou shalt not be afraid for the terror by night; nor for the arrow that flieth by day."** In the present day and age fear is diagnosed as an anxiety disorder or panic attack. However, the Bible tells us in II Timothy 1:7 that fear is a spirit. Fear gets its authority through sin and lack of faith. Fear and depression often accompany each other. A panic attack results when fear is allowed to take precedence over faith. When faith is put into action, it will always overcome fear. Proverbs 29:25 tells us, **"The fear of man bringeth a snare: but whoso putteth his trust in the Lord shall be safe."** Fear is a trap that our mind can become ensnared in. When we choose to trust in God, faith will enter our mind. God's grace, knowledge, wisdom, truth, understanding, judgement, and counsel will keep our mind safe. We will dwell safely in the sound counsel of God, and our mind will be free from the trap of the enemy.

According to scripture, prayer will give us the strength we need to overcome fear because prayer increases our faith. Luke 18:1 says, **"And he spake a parable unto them to this end, that men ought always to pray, and not to faint."** Jesus gave us very good advice. The best thing to do when crisis hits is to pray. Nothing will increase our faith like prayer. Faith weakens the enemy, and his assault on our mind. Prayer is our connection with God. Since God is love, fear is cast out of His presence. The Bible says the perfect love of God will cast out fear. God's love can repair the damage caused by sin.

Therefore, our connection with God through prayer will enable us to overcome fear. The American Psychiatric Association defines a panic attack as the following: "A panic attack is a discrete period in which there is a sudden onset of intense apprehension, fearfulness, or terror, often associated with impending doom. During these attacks, symptoms such as shortness of breath, palpation's, chest pain or discomfort, choking or smothering sensations, and fear of "going crazy" or losing control are present" (361).

When I was diagnosed with panic attacks, I was prescribed Valium. This drug is highly addictive, and I became addicted. It didn't solve the problem because the problem was fear. I have heard it said that fear is the opposite of faith. I can say from personal experience that this is true.

Two, well respected, men of God made these statements concerning fear. T. F. Tenny said, "Fear is the dark room where all your negatives are developed." William Siscoe used this example. "Fear knocked at the door, faith answered, and there was nobody there." There is a lot of truth to these statements. Keep in mind that satan rewards fear like God rewards faith. If you want what is negative, choose fear. If you want what is positive, choose faith. In other words, choose to believe. We are told in II Timothy 1:7, **"For God hath not given us the spirit of fear; but of power, and of love, and of a sound mind."** Let's see what else the Bible has to say, **"There is no fear in love; but perfect love casteth out fear: because fear hath**

torment. He that feareth is not made perfect in love" (I John 4:18).

The word fear translated to Greek means: alarm, fright, be afraid, terror. Looking again at the American Psychiatric Association's definition, we can see similarities between the symptoms for panic attacks, and the Greek definition of fear. The word perfect, used to describe God's love in I John 4:18, signifies a completeness or coming of age. God's love is unconditional. No matter what we do, God does not stop loving us. His love will not keep Him from judging us according to His word, but our actions do not cause Him to stop loving us. In order to receive God's love, we must believe He loves us unconditionally. When we don't believe God loves us, we reject His love. As a result, God's love can't perfect us, cast out fear, or heal us. When we receive God's love, we are receiving Him.

When someone has been hurt or abused by someone they trusted, it can be difficult for them to believe in God's love. We must remember God's love is not the world's love. I John 4:16-17 says, **"And we have known and believed the love that God hath to us. God is love; and he that dwelleth in love dwelleth in God, and God in him. Herein is our love made perfect, that we may have boldness in the day of judgment: because as he is, so are we in this world."** The word dwelleth translated to the Greek language means, abide, continue, dwell, endure, be present, remain, and tarry. These words imply something eternal, not something temporary. If we are consistent in our relationship with God, and continue in His love,

He will dwell in us. When He dwells in us, and we continue to entertain His presence, we can dwell in Him.

As His children, we can come boldly before His throne. Abiding in God's love will perfect us. We will learn to view circumstances and others through God's eyes. When we are born again, we become new creatures in Christ. Romans 6:3-4 says, **"Know ye not, that so many of us as were baptized into Jesus Christ were baptized into his death? Therefore we are buried with him by baptism into death: that like as Christ was raised up from the dead by the glory of the Father, even so we also should walk in newness of life."**

When we are baptized in the name of Jesus Christ, we are actually putting on Christ. We have been buried, and resurrected with Him. The old man dies in the waters of baptism. God wants us to become as He is. We can walk in newness of life by the power of His blood and name. He has put everything He is into the Church for the perfecting of His saints. John 15:13-14 says, **"Greater love hath no man than this, that a man lay down his life for his friends. Ye are my friends, if ye do whatsoever I command you."** Jesus laid down His life for us. That means He must love us very much. We show our love for Him by obeying His commandments.

God doesn't want us to live in fear. Fear is a spirit God has not given us, and we can't allow our minds to be controlled by fear. The enemy will fight against us. He will use circumstances to make us ashamed and afraid. The enemy will attempt to cause division, and try to steal our joy. He wants us to live in fear instead of faith so we won't be effective for God's kingdom.

The Bible says **"Submit yourselves therefore to God. Resist the devil, and he will flee from you" (James 4:7).** By submitting to God's laws in every aspect of our lives, we can make the devil back off. By casting down imaginations, and thinking positive thoughts, we can stop the enemy's onslaught of poison from affecting our mind. The Bible says, **"(For the weapons of our warfare are not carnal, but mighty through God to the pulling down of strongholds;) Casting down imaginations, and every high thing that exalteth itself against the knowledge of God, and bringing into captivity every thought to the obedience of Christ" (II Corinthians 10:4-5).**

Resisting the devil is something that must be done everyday. This scripture tells us the battle is in our mind; we battle with thoughts and imaginations. Our weapons are not carnal (fleshly or physical), but spiritual (through God's spirit), to the pulling down of strongholds, (destroying the enemy's fortresses in our mind). Strongholds are the way we think. We are instructed to control our thoughts by keeping them in obedience to the word of God.

In order to have authority over satan, we must be submitted to God. This means we must live in obedience to the laws of God. We must ignore the thoughts the devil throws our way. Never waste your time listening to the devil. When he sees that you are not effected by his attacks, he will retreat for a season.

When Jesus was in the wilderness, the devil came to Him and tempted Him. When he saw he was getting nowhere, he retreated for a season. The devil will retreat, but he will be back again. However, if we pray for wisdom and stay vigilant in God's word, we will learn to see him coming a mile away. We will know what his tactics are, and we will be able to overcome him. We have been given an offensive weapon. The sword of the spirit, which is the word of God (see Ephesians 6:17). The word has the power to defeat the devil. It is written in John 1:1, **"In the beginning was the Word, and the Word was with God, and the Word was God."** The Bible tells us, **"And the Word was made flesh, and dwelt among us, (and we beheld his glory, the glory as of the only begotten of the Father,) full of grace and truth" (John 1:14).** We know that the one who walked among us was Jesus. John 5:7 says, **"For there are three that bear record in heaven, the Father, the Word, and the Holy Ghost: and these three are one."** Jesus is the almighty God who came to repair the breach between God and man that was caused by sin. He came to heal wounded souls damaged by sin. He came to liberate, and set the oppressed free. He is salvation for all mankind. When we cast down every imagination, bringing our thoughts into obedience to the word. Jesus who is truth will make us free. Our obedience to the truth of the gospel will deliver us, and a relationship with Jesus Christ will be our salvation.

The Answer

Where there is void, confusion, and disorder,

You speak calmness, peace and order.

Where there is darkness, you speak light.

Where there is death you speak life.

Where there is want, you make wine

Where there are sinners, you would dine

Where there is need of knowledge, you have supplied.

There in your word the wisdom of the ages resides.

Where there is a repentant heart, you draw near.

To blind eyes you give sight, you make deaf ears hear.

Where there is a soul that longs to be free,

You break every yoke, you alone have the key.

There in your word, the truth we will find.

Your wisdom we desire, control of our mind.

There is no one like you, everlasting mercy you have shown,

The answer is to know you, the oil of joy to those who mourn.

Chapter Three

The Oil of Joy for Mourning

There are things that happen to us in life that shouldn't have happened to anyone. There are two ways we can react to life's circumstances. One option is to let them destroy our character, make us bitter, and allow them to determine our destiny. Our other option is to give the situation to God, and allow Him to determine our destiny. When we give our bad circumstances to God, He will use them to make us stronger and give us a testimony. Jesus can take something meant for evil and use it for good. The Bible gives us an example of this in chapter 37 of the book of Genesis.

Joseph's brothers were jealous, and wanted to get rid of him. Instead of killing him, they threw him in a pit. Judah, one of his brothers, suggested selling him. Joseph was sold to some Ishmeelites, and as a result, Joseph ended up as a slave in Egypt. In Egypt Joseph was accused falsely by Pharaoh's wife who had attempted to seduce him. He was thrown in prison for two years, but he kept his integrity. In the end, God took what Joseph's brothers meant for evil, and turned his bad circumstance into something good.

Joseph was appointed as a ruler in Egypt second only to Pharaoh. He saved his family, and the lives of many others. God can take what seems to be the worst thing that could happen to us, turn the situation around, and use it as a testimony that can help others. Perhaps our testimony will change their lives. The following story is true. It is shared for the purpose of enlightening the reader to the need for God in every aspect of our lives. We need His perfect love and law to make us complete. I know from personal experience that God can turn our mistakes and failures into testimonies.

There was a boy who was very intelligent. From the time he was a small child he understood math, science, and geography beyond his years. His mother was young, came from a dysfunctional family, and was married at age 16. He had one sister who was three years older than him. She loved him, and looked out for him. After six years of marriage, their parents divorced. Before the divorce, their parents fought often. The children witnessed their father verbally abusing, and beating their mother many times. The circumstances that lead to the divorce were traumatic.

One night, after severely beating their mother, their father left. They didn't see him again for approximately two years. To make matters worse, their mother was always depressed. It was very difficult to make ends meet. Also, she was angry with their father. Her front tooth had been knocked out, and her nose had been broken. It was humiliating for her to work, and to be seen in public places. Unfortunately, she didn't realize how severely the trauma had affected her children. She didn't realize that she wasn't giving them what they needed to make them feel loved and secure.

After two years, their father came back into their lives. He would come and take them for the weekend. Then he remarried, moved, and quit coming to see them all together. When it was the boy's birthday, he kept checking the mailbox. He would say "I know my dad will send me something for my birthday." Nothing ever came. This was very hard for the boy. His mother felt bad for him, and she didn't know what to do. Her anger towards their father increased and unfortunately she let it show. She was hurt from the divorce and the abuse. She didn't realize the children were picking up on the anger and rejection she felt. She had never learned parenting skills, and she didn't have a relationship with Jesus. She knew of Him, but didn't know Him. She found out years later, there is a big difference between knowing of Jesus and truly knowing Him.

The boy would see his mother weeping over financial difficulties and other problems. He would ask her, "mom, why don't you pray?" His mother would pray for him and his sister at bedtime. Something inside the boy knew this was the answer. Unfortunately, she was preoccupied with worrying about finances, school, and work. She never took the time to respond to that question or consider it. She was unhappy, and focused on negative things instead of looking at positive things. Hoping to improve herself and the way she felt, she became involved in running. She participated in local 10k races and marathons. The children were involved in after school activities. They were in karate and music lessons.

These activities didn't help them with the problems they were having. She wasn't aware that anger and depression were being passed down to her children. To make matters worse, the boy and his sister never had a positive male role model. The men that their mother became involved with were a negative influence. Their mother took them to denominational Churches because she went as a child, and it was a tradition to go. However, it never made a real difference in their lives.

The boy grew angrier as the years went on. He felt he was different from the kids at school. Many of his friends had fathers, and lived in nice houses. His mother would buy things for the children in an effort to show them she loved them. Unfortunately, this taught them that material things and money were important. As time went by the boy developed worse behavior problems.

His mother took him to two facilities to receive counseling, but they couldn't help. They asked, "what is it you would like us to do for your son?" If his mother had known the answer, she would have done it for him herself. His mother went to counselors for her depression, and was asked similar questions. How could she tell them the answer? The reason she went to them was because she was looking for answers. Years later, she found that the answer to every problem is in the word of God.

One summer the boy was in camp. The camp leader called his mother, and told her he had vandalized the bus. The same day, the baby sitter told her she was having problems controlling him. The camp leader suggested that he be evaluated at Mercy Center. His mother didn't know what else to do. She thought she was doing the best thing for him, and hoped that they could help him. The man in charge at Mercy Center told her that if she didn't do something, he would end up in prison.

He became angry and combative at Mercy Center. He was sent from Mercy Center to Singer. Singer is an institution for people with mental illness. The boy was admitted to the children's ward. It was hard for his mother to leave him there. She didn't want to. The boy told her that she was doing it because she didn't love him. She had him stay because she thought it was the best thing for him. Everyone told her it was. Singer diagnosed the boy with Attention-Deficit/Hyperactivity Disorder. He stayed at Singer for the summer, and part of the next school year. While he was there, he was given a standard IQ test. The results showed that he scored in the top 3% in the nation. The administrator told his mother, "you have no idea how smart this kid is." His mother was confused. He was very intelligent, but had all these behavior problems. It didn't make any sense.

Unfortunately, his transition back to public school was difficult. He was functioning in grade levels above the other children in his class. He was supposed to be given higher level work. Instead he was given the same work as the other students. His mother made an attempt to resolve the situation with the department in charge of special education, but received no help from them. The end result was that he was labeled as a special education student, and given the same curriculum as other students his age. He had been doing college level curriculum at Singer. When he had to repeat the work over again, he became frustrated and angry.

He had been prescribed medication for ADHD at Singer. The drugs prescribed were Dexedrine and Ritalin. He was still on Ritalin when he came home. These drugs made no difference in his behavior. He complained of headaches, and looked sad all the time. His mother took him off the Ritalin after he came home. The boy continued into adulthood to become an angry young man.

The boy in the previous story is my son. I wish these things never happened. I wish everything had been different. It could have been, if I had known and applied the word of God to our lives. I wish I had understood the importance of prayer, and having the power of the word of God in our lives. Everything would have been different. I wouldn't have lived the way I did. I wish I had thought about the question my son asked, "mom, why don't you pray?" While we shouldn't dwell on our past mistakes, we can use them to help someone else. This is why I feel it is so important to tell this story, and let others know what Jesus has delivered me from. I want others to know that the word of God is truth and life. His truth has changed my life. A difference can be made in our lives, and any child's behavior, when we apply Biblical principles.

Many children today are receiving the label ADHD. Labels are very damaging to children because they may feel they don't fit in with others or they may believe they are bad. They may grow up believing they have an excuse for their behavior. It is also possible that they might carry the belief they are flawed into adulthood. As a result, they may become adults who believe they are not responsible for their own behavior.

If a child has already been diagnosed with ADHD, God's word still works. It's never too late to change the way we have been doing things and start over. We should be honest with our children, and be willing to admit when we have made mistakes. We should let our children know that we want to change the way things are because we love them. It will not hurt our image to admit we don't know everything. When we are willing to admit we are wrong, our children will learn to do the same. Sometimes our children need to see a change in us before they can change. God's word works whenever it is applied and followed. No one can restore a life and self-esteem like Jesus can. There is no one like Him. He cares about us, and wants to help us raise our children. I know from personal experience that labels adversely affect a child's self-esteem. I suffered a serious head injury as a child. Although I didn't have brain damage, I felt I was different than other children my age.

When I was four, I was kicked in the head by a horse. I was in a coma for two days and wasn't expected to live. It is because of the grace of God, and my family's prayers that I am alive. My Grandma told me she prayed all night begging God to spare my life. She said that when God healed me, she knew He had a plan for me. Although God healed me, I strayed away from God, as I became an adult. During the years I was lost, my Grandma said she asked God why this had happened. She has told me recently that now she understands why. God answers prayer, but not always in the way we think He will.

I know that there is a greater purpose behind the things that happen in our lives. Because of this accident, I understand how a label can make a child feel. The injury caused a bone chip to enter the cerebral cortex of my brain, which the surgeon removed. I became right-handed instead of left-handed. I was still able to function, but I always felt different. I remember I was taken to a doctor sometime after the accident. It seemed very important to him that I remember what had happened before the accident. At one point he was yelling at me, telling me to think about it so I could remember. I felt that he was angry with me. I was scared and couldn't remember anything. Eventually the memory did come back to me.

My parents were always worried I would hit my head, and I was restricted from certain activities. Many times I felt left out, but now I understand my parents concern. The point I want to make is that I always felt different. I felt like there was something wrong with me. This is how a label can affect the way a child feels about themself.

In the DSM-IV-TR, the American Psychiatric Association gives the following diagnostic criteria to diagnose ADHD:

> The essential feature of Attention Deficit/Hyperactivity Disorder is a persistent pattern of inattention and/or hyperactivity-impulsivity that is more frequently displayed and more severe than is typically observed in individuals at a comparable level of development (criterion A). Some hyperactive impulsive or inattentive symptoms that cause impairment must have been present before the age of 7 years, although many individuals are diagnosed after the symptoms have been present for a number of years, especially in the case of individuals with the Predominately Inattentive type (criterion B). Some impairment from the symptoms must be present in at least two settings (e.g. at home and school or work) (criterion C). There must be a clear evidence

of interference with developmentally appropriate social, academic, or occupational functioning (criterion D).

The DSM-IV-TR gives these symptoms as associated features of this disorder:

Associated features vary depending on age and developmental stage and may include low frustration tolerance, temper outbursts, bossiness, stubbornness, excessive and frequent insistence that requests be met, mood liability, demoralization, dysphoria, rejection by peers, and poor self-esteem. Academic achievement is often markedly impaired, and devalued, typically leading to conflict with the family and school authorities. A substantial proportion (approximately half) of clinic referred children with Attention Deficit/Hyperactivity Disorder also have Oppositional Defiant Disorder or Conduct Disorder (87-88).

The DSM-IV-TR states, "There are no laboratory tests, neurological assessments, or attentional assessments that have been established as diagnostic in the clinical assessment of Attention-Deficit/Hyperactivity Disorder" (88-89). The diagnosis of ADHD, its criterion, and it features are based on man's theory. They have even given defiant behavior a label, including it as a separate disorder.

The American Psychiatric Association states that ADHD has a familiar pattern. These behaviors can be inherited, but also can be brought on by traumatic experiences. These may include physical or sexual abuse, divorce, and living in a dysfunctional household. Another cause is lack of sound, Biblical, discipline.

Behavior problems can also be rooted in anger and unforgiveness. For example, my son's behavior problems manifested after my divorce from an abusive marriage. Both children suffered from their father's rejection; matters were made worse by growing up in an unstable environment.

To add to these problems, my son inherited a strong will. It is a fact that behaviors can be inherited or learned. Inappropriate thought processes, and negative things we say or do can be passed down to our children. Also, we are all born with a fallen nature. Lack of proper example and teaching contributed to these behavior problems. Children should be taught right and wrong from a Biblical standpoint from the time they are old enough to know right from wrong. Parents must set the example. I wish I had realized how closely my children paid attention to my actions.

Also, It has been medically proven that inappropriate behavior can be a result of the diet a child is eating. Low blood sugar and food allergies can adversely effect a child's behavior. Also, there are differences in learning styles. This should be taken into consideration if the child's problems seem to be worse at school. Some children may have learning difficulties, or disabilities that are not addressed. These may cause anger and frustration during school.

It is very important to get to the root of the problem and work on solving it. We mustn't attempt to cover behavior problems with medication. Although medication may temporarily cover the problem, in the long run it doesn't solve the problem. Medicating children will teach them to seek the help of drugs or products to solve their problems instead of seeking God. God did not intend for us to use medication to control our children. He gives us instruction in His word on how to raise children properly. Children need training, and they need their parent's time and attention.

They should be loved, disciplined, and made to feel they are important. Most importantly, they should be taught to know Jesus. They should be encouraged to pray and learn the word of God. Parents should pray, and spend time reading God's word to their children. If they see their parents doing these things, they will learn to do them as well. We learn from watching our parents. They should be taught to go to Church, and to take their problems to Jesus. Children should be taught to deal with situations that come their way from a Biblical perspective. Parents should set an example and do the same.

Jesus tells us to bring children to Him. Mark 10:14 says, **"...Suffer the little children to come unto me, and forbid them not: for of such is the kingdom of God."** Children are a gift from God. His word gives us guidelines for proper training and discipline of children. One of the problems we see today is that children aren't properly disciplined. God's word tells us not to withhold discipline from a child (Proverbs 23:13).

The Bible also says, **"Thou shalt beat him with the rod, and shalt deliver his soul from hell" (Proverbs 23:14).** These scriptures are not telling parents to beat their children in a way that is abusive. This scripture is saying that discipline will keep a child from doing what is wrong. The purpose of spanking a child is so he will associate doing what is wrong with pain and turn away from sin. Discipline should always be carried out in love. Biblical discipline is designed to keep the child from turning towards a life of sin. A child will find security in the boundaries set by his or her parents. When children are not taught right from wrong, they make poor choices that negatively effect their lives.

A price will always be paid for violating God's word. Unfortunately, the children suffer the consequences more than the parents do. **Proverbs 22:6 says, "Train up a child in the way he should go: and when he is old, he will not depart from it." Parents shouldn't leave their children to their own devices. The Bible tells us, "Foolishness is bound in the heart of a child; but the rod of correction shall drive it far from him" (Proverbs 22:15).** Although there is scripture that teaches corporal punishment, there is also scripture that teaches us that everything must be done in love. Never wait until you are angry to spank or discipline. Parents should never slap their children on the face or humiliate them in front of others.

We need to break old patterns that we have learned and form new ones. If a person grew up in a house where there was yelling, they will have a tendency to yell at their children. If they were beaten or disciplined in anger, they will often discipline their children in this manner. However, some go in the opposite direction and won't discipline their children at all. This is equally as damaging. These patterns must be broken because they provoke a child to anger. If these patterns are not broken, they will be passed to the next generation. Lack of proper discipline is the reason for dysfunction in many families because if children aren't properly disciplined, they don't learn how to properly discipline their own children. We mustn't allow the enemy to pass abuse, dysfunction, and iniquity to the next generation.

We must teach our children by example, learning and obeying the word of God. Then our children will understand why they are expected to live by God's laws. When they know God's laws they will understand that they should obey their parents. The Bible tells us, **"Children, obey your parents in all things: for this is well pleasing unto the Lord" (Colossians 3:20). Colossians 3:21 tells us, "Fathers, provoke not your children to anger, lest they be discouraged."**

Again, children should be disciplined in a way that does not provoke them to anger, humiliate or discourage them. They should be given consistent boundaries so they know what to expect. It is important to set aside time to spend with your children, and talk with them about how they feel. Whenever appropriate, be open with your children and communicate your feelings to them. Communication is important in any relationship. Communicating to our children what we have learned about life gives them valuable information. We can tell our children what we have learned from our past mistakes, and what we would do if we had it to do over again. It is possible that our children will learn from our mistakes.

We must get beyond the mentality of shame associated with our past mistakes when we communicate with our children. Shame is a grudge we hold against ourselves. Shame is a form of unforgiveness that is damaging to our relationships with others. Shame can prevent us from being open or admitting we have made mistakes, but it's never too late to change our way of thinking. Everyday we have the chance to live in liberty by God's principles. When our children see a change in us, it will have a positive effect on them regardless of their age. We can't let shame control our emotions or actions. All of us have done things we regret, but it is likely that our mistakes have brought us to a place of repentance and salvation.

Our greatest help or hindrance is the way we choose to think. We must choose not to dwell on past mistakes, even if they have adversely affected our children. It is not necessary to spend large amounts of money on family counseling when we look into the riches of God's word. Jesus took upon Himself the shame of the whole world when He paid the price for every imaginable sin. Money cannot buy the liberty that was afforded to us at Calvary. The book of Revelation enlightens us to the true riches available to all through Jesus Christ. The Church of Laodecia was increased with goods, and believed they had need of nothing. According to Jesus, they were poor, wretched, miserable, blind, and naked (see Revelation 3:17).

Since their focus was on money and material things, Jesus spoke to them in terms they could understand. He counseled them to purchase what they needed to overcome their spiritual poverty. Revelation 3:18 says, "I counsel thee to buy of me gold tried in the fire, that thou mayest be rich; and white raiment, that thou mayest be clothed, and that the shame of thy nakedness do not appear; and anoint thine eyes with eye-salve, that thou mayest see." History tells us that "Laodecia had a famous medical college where 'Phrygian powder' was used to make eyesalve" (Stearn 801).

However, they chose to depend on the things of this world, and remained spiritually blind. Jesus encourages us to invest in His riches, not the cheap things of this world that soon become corrupted. He has been tried in the greatest fiery trial, and has come through as pure gold. He has assured us that Calvary is more than enough, and has conquered shame. When we are baptized in Jesus name, we wear a new garment. Our sins are washed away, and God only sees His righteousness. The spirit of the Lord will anoint our eyes so we will be able to see, and comprehend the power of His forgiveness.

When our actions have had a negative effect on our children, it can be difficult to forgive ourselves. It has been a struggle for me to forgive myself for my failures concerning my children. During a time of great difficulty I asked Jesus to remove the shame I felt. He answered me saying, "I already have, but you don't believe it." At that point I realized what we believe is the deciding factor in our ability to overcome. We must choose to believe Jesus loves and forgives us. Also, it is important that our children know we believe this. Our children will know what we believe because it will show in our actions. When we believe in the love of God towards us, it makes a difference in the way we speak and act. We must allow God to heal our wounded spirits, and we must teach our children about the love of God. If we allow our children to learn from psychiatrists or counselors that don't know the truth of the gospel, we are doing them harm.

Currently, my main source of income is housecleaning. While I was cleaning a house for a client, I heard something on television that caught my attention. I went into the other room to catch the end of a special on Good Morning America. There was a psychologist from Dartmouth University discussing the results of a study performed on children with emotional and behavioral problems. The study revealed that these children showed marked improvement in their behavior when they were involved in Church, and activities related to religion. She stated that children appear to have a need for involvement in activities related to religion. She also stated that parents might be doing their children psychological harm by not having them involved in religion.

It seems that some areas of psychology are beginning to realize what the Bible has taught us all along. The Bible tells us that God created mankind as a spiritual being. He created every human with a basic need for a relationship with the God that created him. The Bible teaches us that we are made up of body, soul, and spirit. Therefore, every human is a spiritual being that has spiritual needs. When these needs are not met in God's intended way, man will attempt to fill these needs in his own way. The enemy offers many alternatives to God's intended way. Some of these alternatives are gangs, drugs, material things, immoral sexual relationships, and much more. Modern psychology may not understand this need from a Biblical standpoint, but they are beginning to see the importance of fulfilling the needs of the spiritual man.

When Jesus is brought into any situation, it gets better. He is an ever-present help in time of need. Church involvement is important for the health of our spiritual man. We are told in scripture that we should belong to the body of Christ, which is the Church. However, we must be sure that the Church we attend teaches the truth of the gospel. Paul writes, **"But though we, or an angel from heaven, preach any other gospel unto you than that which we have preached unto you, let him be accursed" (Galatians 1:8).** We must stay in God's word, and many religions do not. It is vitally important to our salvation to find a Church that teaches the gospel according to the scripture. The Bible warns us not to add to or to subtract from God's word. There are warnings of severe consequences to those who do (see Deuteronomy 4:2, Proverbs 30:5-6, Revelation 22:18-19).

We must base all our beliefs on the word of God. He has the power to change any situation, and He is greater than any circumstance. I can testify to this because He has changed my life for the better. Even though my son is not presently living for God, I know that with God all things are possible. I believe in God's appointed time, my son will do great things for Him. I believe in the power of prayer, and I believe in the power of Jesus. Since I have been living for God my relationship with my son has improved, and he is not as angry as he once was.

It is never too late for Jesus to perform a miracle in someone's life. For those that have small children, I encourage you to raise them to know and reverence God. We are living in perilous times. Paul warns the Church in II Timothy 3:2, **"For men shall be lovers of their own selves, covetous, boasters, proud, blasphemers, disobedient to parents, unthankful, unholy."** None of us want this to be said of our children. We do not want them to grow up to be lost. Don't allow them to believe they have an excuse for their bad behavior. We can't allow our children be labeled or drugged, and we can't allow them to believe that bad behavior is acceptable. At Wings conference, Gayla Foster gave this acronym for ADHD: Awareness, Discipline, Healthy Living, and Devotion. I have expanded on her acronym.

Awareness - We should be aware of what is going on with our children. Many times children will act out if they are disturbed about something. Spend time talking to the child to find out if something happened that is the root cause of the behavior. Perhaps something happened at school or something may be going on in the home that has upset the child. Parents should watch for signs of abuse, and questions should be asked if abuse is suspected. Take into consideration where the child spends his or her day and with whom.

Parents of children diagnosed with ADHD should be aware that according to Dr. Mary Block, ADHD has become an industry. Dr. Block, author of the book, ***No More Ritalin***, and founder of the Block Center in Texas, makes these statements:

There certainly seems to be many more children diagnosed with ADHD today than 20 years ago. Today, ADHD has grown into an industry. Doctors, pharmaceutical companies, psychologists, psychiatrists, neurologists, pediatricians, family practitioners, tutors, and schools all own a piece of this industry. Once a major American industry exists, it just keeps on growing. With the industry driving the market, the goal is no longer to fix the problem, but to continue to treat the symptoms. This process generates money for those in the industry. If you fix the problems creating the symptoms, all the revenue-producing drugs and services would go away. There would be no need for them.

Our adversary uses the label ADHD, and man's love of money to destroy lives. We mustn't let our children become his victims. The Bible calls the love of money "the root of all evil." We mustn't allow the label ADHD to be placed on our children by a psychiatrist or society. As has been previously stated, there are no laboratory findings to support the existence of ADHD. The diagnosis is made based on man's theory. According to Dr. Block, a diagnosis is often made on the basis of an individual's point of view:

Look closely at the actual wording of DSM-IV diagnosis. The symptoms of ADHD are highly subjective. The chance that your child will or will not receive a diagnosis of ADHD depends upon the point of view of the individual making the evaluation. If the evaluator believes that a child should be seen and not heard and should be able to remain seated for long periods of time, then the child is more likely to receive an ADHD diagnosis.

Parents should be aware that the drugs used to treat ADHD have harmful side effects. Dr. Block lists some of the known side effects of the drug Ritalin:

Ritalin has been used for many years, so we are very familiar with the short-term side-effects of that drug. The known short-term side-effects of Ritalin include loss of appetite, decreased growth, tics, visual disturbances, nervousness, insomnia, depression, social withdrawal, irritability, abdominal pain, increased heart rate, and psychotic-like symptoms. Again, these are the side effects of short-term use. Since long-term use is a relatively new phenomenon, the long term side-effects have yet to be discovered.

Breggin and Cohen further elaborate on the dangers of giving stimulants to children:

> We are appalled by the widespread use of stimulants to control and suppress the behavior of children diagnosed ADHD. The aim is to correct behavior described in terms of hyperactivity, impulsivity, and inattention. In actuality, however, stimulants subdue behavior by impairing mental function; they often cause the very problems they are supposed to correct. Ritalin and amphetamines have almost identical adverse effects. Stimulants have a powerful impact on the functioning of the brain and mind. They can lead to addiction and abuse. Children may give away or sell their stimulants to older children. Parents may illegally use or sell their children's Ritalin or amphetamine. In many or most children, stimulants routinely cause rebound, involving a worsening of behavioral symptoms a few hours after the last dose. And especially with larger or more prolonged dosing, this can lead to severe withdrawal reactions such as "crashing," which is characterized by extreme fatigue, depression, and even suicidal feelings. Stimulants can also cause the following: excessive stimulation of the brain, including

insomnia and seizures; agitation, irritability, and nervousness; confusion and disorientation; personality changes; apathy, social isolation, sadness, and very commonly depression. The most characteristic toxic psychosis from stimulants is mania. In addition, stimulants can cause paranoia, involving fearful and even violent feelings toward others. Stimulants such as Ritalin have been used in experiments to worsen the symptoms of patients labeled schizophrenic—a practice that should be considered unethical. Ritalin causes liver cancer in rats, but this outcome has not been reported in humans. Furthermore, stimulants can cause a variety of emotional disturbances that are mistakenly considered "therapeutic", including flattened emotions and robotic behavior. Children who take these drugs frequently lose the sparkle in their eyes. The edge comes off their creativity and vitality. Some become zombie-like. When stimulants cause compliance, obedience, reduced intuitive, reduced autonomy, they make children easier to manage. But these "therapeutic" effects, such as compliance or increased obedience, should be viewed as adverse drug effects.

All stimulants can cause the very symptoms they are supposed to treat, hyperactivity, loss of impulse control, and diminished concentration and focus. They can worsen a child or adult's reaction to stress or anxiety. Stimulants also cause dizziness, headache, insomnia, palpitations, abnormally increased heart rate, increased blood pressure, cardiac arrhythmias, (heart attack due to arrhythmias have been reported to the FDA); loss of appetite, weight loss, nausea, vomiting, constipation, and stomach pain; dry mouth; blurred vision; abnormal liver function; muscle cramping; tremor; hair loss; itching; and scratching; severe and life-threatening skin eruptions; bleeding problems; weakened immunity; growth hormone disruption and prolactin hormone disruption. Permanent tics, sometimes categorized as Tourette's syndrome, are a serious complication. They often start in the face and neck (65-66). The stimulant Ritalin disrupts growth hormone production, inhibiting the growth of the child's brain while creating severe biochemical imbalances within it. Indeed, there is evidence that stimulants can cause lasting harm to the brain. From our perspective, these dangers constitute too high a risk for any child to pay. We believe that these drugs should never be given to children (103).

Parents should also be aware that Ritalin is a controlled substance, which is cocaine like in its makeup. "Both drugs use the same receptor site in the brain, give the same high and in medical research are used interchangeably. The only difference appears to be that cocaine leaves the receptor site more quickly, possibly making it more addictive" (Block 30). Although there are new drugs on the market for ADHD, it is not possible to know what the long-term side effects of these drugs might be. These drugs have the potential to cause harm physically and spiritually. God's way is the best way for our children.

Discipline - Again, those who weren't properly disciplined by their parents often have difficulty disciplining their children. We don't have to let what happened in our past carry over into our children's future. It's never too late to take the appropriate steps to change negative behavior. We must make every effort to act in a positive manner. Keeping in mind that the word of God is positive. Although we live in a negative world with negative influences, we have a positive God. He gives us direction, answers, and guidelines to follow in His word. The Bible says, **"Chasten thy son while there is hope, and let not thy soul spare for his crying" (Proverbs 19:18).** While we might feel cruel when we punish our children, the Bible says that there is hope in doing so. We can't let memories from past abuse interfere with healthy, Biblical, discipline.

Proverbs 29:17 says, **"Correct thy son, and he shall give thee rest; yea, he shall give delight unto thy soul."** The Bible also says that withholding discipline from your child is akin to hating him. **"He that spareth his rod hateth his son: but he that loveth him chasteneth him betimes" (Proverbs 13:24).** We learn from these scriptures that God wants us to discipline our children. Although children should be treated equally, some children are more headstrong than others, and require more discipline. No matter the situation, a child needs instruction and guidance. **"The rod and reproof give wisdom: but a child left to himself bringeth his mother to shame" (Proverbs 29:15).** Children should not be left to their own devices, and must be taught that there will be consequences for their behavior. They should be taught that you will reap what you sow.

Healthy Living - Good nutrition is important for everyone. What we eat affects our behavior because it affects how we feel. Many processed foods are loaded with sugar, hydrogenated fats, and preservatives. Many have little or no nutritional value. There are chemical additives in many foods. We don't know what the effects of some of these chemicals might be. It is best to read labels when shopping, and leave foods containing unknown ingredients on the store shelf. Simple, whole foods are the best foods. In Bible times, God's people ate simple foods, such as, fruits, nuts, vegetables, grains, lentils, dairy, and meat. Considering the time and conditions they lived in, they were reasonably healthy.

Today, almost every drink on the market has sugar in it. There is also sugar added to most processed foods. Many children eat too much sugar, and become hyperactive as a result. Also, beware of hydrogenated oils known as Trans fats. These are in many prepared foods. These are man-made fats, and have been linked to coronary artery disease. According to Dr. Block, many children diagnosed with ADHD have an underlying health problem. She makes this statement, "Looking for the underlying cause of a problem will often lead to nutrition since nutrition underlies every way the body works. The body cannot function properly without the right nutrients. Looking for the underlying cause takes a knowledge and understanding of how the body works beyond the obvious symptoms. Finding the underlying cause of a problem and fixing it is the only way to achieve long-term results" (Block 69-70).

Dr. Block states that low blood sugar (hypoglycemia) is the most significant problem she finds in the treatment of children with behavioral problems:

The child who is agitated or irritable when he or she wakes up in the morning or before meals and then better after eating is probably effected by hypoglycemia. The child with the Jekyll and Hyde behavior, who is sweet and fine one minute and then for no apparent reason is agitated, angry, and irritable the next may have hypoglycemia. Hypoglycemia or low blood sugar occurs when our bloodstream does not have an adequate amount of sugar in it. This can occur in at least two different ways. One way is not to eat frequently enough. All of our foods eventually breakdown and convert to sugar, or glucose, in the body. If we don't eat frequently enough, there is not a continuous supply of sugar going into the bloodstream. The second way to get low blood sugar is to eat sugar or foods high in sugar content. This may appear paradoxical. It would seem if you ate sugar it would cause more sugar to go into the bloodstream, not less. However, some people have "reactive hypoglycemia." Reactive hypoglycemia can occur after ingesting refined carbohydrates, foods high in sugar, or alcohol. If you eat a lot of refined carbohydrates, the sugar goes into your bloodstream very quickly (74-76).

Food allergies are another cause of behavioral problems in children. This is Bart's story:

Bart had been prescribed several different drugs for his behavior. None of them were effective. He was hospitalized for his behavior problems in a psychiatric institution twice by the age of five. When his insurance ran out, he was discharged. His symptoms continued. Bart's parents brought him to see me, and I tested him for allergies and sensitivities. When I tested Bart for sensitivity to dairy products, his psychotic symptoms exhibited themselves with a vengeance. Bart became aggressive, angry, and combative. He threatened to hit his mother and attempted to run out of the office. He kicked and tried to bite his mother when she stopped him. We had identified the irritant. (Block 83)

Other factors may have been contributing to this child's behavior problems, but one obvious problem was a food allergy. We must take the appropriate steps to discover the root cause of behavior problems. They cannot, and will not be solved with drugs. What we eat really does affect the way we feel. We must feed our spiritual and physical man a healthy diet.

According to Natural Health Practitioner George Moore, who has twelve years experience in the natural health field, the word of God has healing power. George has performed numerous health and wellness consultations and seminars. When I spoke with him during a consultation, He quoted Psalm 107:20 saying, "He sent his word, and healed them, and delivered them from their destructions." He also made the following statement, "Those who are in the word of God always do better than those who rely only on natural means."

Devotion - Children need love and devotion. They need to know that they are important, and that their thoughts and feelings matter. It is important to spend time with your children. Get involved in reading, playing games, and other activities with your children. Don't allow the television to baby-sit your children. John Rosemond, a family psychologist from Indiana, writes a column in the Richmond Times-dispatch. He gives the testimony of a woman who took television away from her four children. At first the children whined they were bored. She told them she would give them jobs to do. After one week, they were entertaining themselves.

These are some of the effects of television according to research done by psychologist Jane Healy ("The Endangered Mind", "Failure to connect"). Television contributes to Learning disabilities, heightened aggressive tendencies, under achievement, and mood swings. According to Healy, video and computer games are equally as damaging.

I have recently heard statistics that are very disturbing. In 1990 there were approximately 27 references made to sex per hour on regular television. As of the year 2000, the references made to sex increased to 220 per hour. Also in 1990 85% of young people polled felt that homosexuality was wrong. As of the year 2000, 75% felt that it was all right, and some even said it was healthy. Children learn a lot of unhealthy things from television. They will also pick up things from school, and exposure to everyday life. Some of these things can't be prevented, but what they watch on television can be monitored. Let them know that you love them enough to care about what they are watching, and what they are doing.

The Bible tells us to pass our heritage down to our children. When the children of Israel crossed over the river Jordan into the land God promised them, God parted the waters for them to cross as He did at the Red Sea. God told Joshua to command the men among them to gather twelve stones out of the Jordan, one for each tribe of Israel. These stones were then piled on the other side of the Jordan. He commanded them to do this so when their children asked what the stones meant, they would be able to tell them all that God had done for them. The Bible says:

And He spake unto the children of Israel, saying, When your children shall ask their fathers in time to come, saying, What mean these stones? Then ye shall let your children know, saying, Israel came over this Jordan on dry land. For the Lord your God dried up the waters of Jordan from before you, until ye were passed over, as the Lord your God did to the Red sea, which he dried up from before us, until we were gone over: That all the people of the earth might know the hand of the Lord, that it is mighty: that ye might fear the Lord your God for ever. (Joshua 4:21-24)

God wants us to tell our children of the great things He has done in our lives, and to teach them to fear and reverence Him. We should tell them of His goodness and mercy, and all He has done for us. He is a redeemer, a healer, and a provider, and so much more. We should tell them that although He is a God of love, He is also a God of judgement. The Bible says that there rose up a generation that knew not God. We must protect the future generations. We must take the time to teach our children about Jesus. It's not likely the world will.

Whatever the situation, no matter how bad it seems, the situation can be turned around. The saddest situation can be changed when Jesus enters in. He can soften the hardest heart, and He can remove doubt and fear when He draws near. Some children are strong-willed. The older they get, the harder it can be. Stay close to Jesus because all things are possible with God. No matter what happens, we can take our problems to Jesus. Weeping may last for the night, but joy will come in the morning. Jesus will comfort all those who mourn with the anointing oil of the Holy Ghost. By the power of His spirit, we can receive peace and understanding in times of doubt and fear.

The Purchase

Man sat in darkness, no hope of his own.

Bound up in prison, he seemed so alone.

Because of transgression, man made the wrong choice.

Man could no longer hear God's voice.

God in His mercy had a plan in mind,

A cure for transgression, from the beginning of time.

A purchase was made with blood so pure,

Of merchandise damaged by the prince of this world.

The God of heaven, eternal and divine,

Saw man's plight as He looked down through time.

The God of heaven stepped down and became man,

All in accordance with His perfect plan.

To repair the damage caused by sin.

To make it possible for man to commune with Him again.

When man is forgiven, and repents of bitterness,

He then will be free of all strife and malice.

Man no longer has to live bound by sin.

Man can choose to forgive, and he will be forgiven.

Chapter Four

The Vengeance of Our God

"Say to them that are of a fearful heart, Be strong, fear not: behold, your God will come with vengeance, even God with a recompense; he will come and save you" (Isaiah 35:4). We must believe this promise. God has promised us that He will come to our rescue. We must wait on God during trials, and when others have done us wrong. We must believe that God will do as He promised. When we attempt to avenge ourselves, taking vengeance into our own hands, we are violating the word of God. Romans 12:19 says, **"Dearly beloved, avenge not yourselves, but rather give place unto wrath: for it is written, Vengeance is mine; I will repay, saith the Lord."** I once heard a well respected man of God say, "Glory and vengeance are God's, don't mess with either." This is very good advice. Another word often used for holding vengeance is unforgiveness. The Bible calls holding vengeance or unforgiveness bitterness. Unforgiveness is one of the greatest spiritual problems that mankind faces today.

The Bible tells us that we must forgive. The freedom of forgiveness was one of the most powerful revelations I received after becoming a Christian. In fact, forgiveness is the basis for Christianity. Those who refuse to forgive will eventually backslide, and will live in torment. This shouldn't surprise us because refusing to forgive goes directly against the word of God. During prayer God inspired me with this thought, "Whosoever refuses to forgive is an enemy of the cross. The cross is all about forgiveness." We should make it a practice to include forgiveness in our daily prayer meeting. Jesus said, **"And when ye stand praying, forgive, if ye have aught against any: that your Father also which is in heaven may forgive you your trespasses. But if ye do not forgive, neither will your Father which is in heaven forgive your trespasses" (Mark 11:25 - 26).** Jesus also said, **"And forgive us our debts, as we forgive our debtors" (Matthew 6:12).**

In the next verses that follow, Jesus admonishes us again to forgive. **"For if ye forgive men their trespasses, your heavenly Father will also forgive you: But if ye forgive not men their trespasses, neither will your Father forgive your trespasses" (Mathew 6:14-15).** Forgiveness is vital to our salvation as well as our overall well being, both spiritual and physical. If we are to recover our mind from the snare of the devil we, must forgive. We cannot be delivered without forgiveness. Jesus said:

Woe to the world because of offenses! for it must needs be that offenses come; but woe to that man by whom the offense cometh! Wherefore if thy hand or foot offend thee, cut them off, and cast them from thee: it is better for thee to enter life halt or maimed, rather than having two hands or two feet to be cast into everlasting fire. And if thine eye offend thee, pluck it out, and cast it from thee: it is better for thee to enter into life with one eye, rather than having two eyes to be cast into hell fire (Matthew 18:7-9).

Jesus is not telling us to literally cut off parts of our body because that would not save us from hell. He is telling us that no matter what the cost, cut off all offense. It is better to lose our carnal attitude, and way of thinking, than it is for us to be cast into hell with them. According to this scripture we will not enter eternal life with harbored offence, but Jesus tells us offenses will come. Given this knowledge, we must learn the appropriate way to deal with offense when it comes our way.

The Bible gives us guidelines for dealing with offense in Matthew 18:15-17. If our brother trespasses against us, we are to go to him alone and tell him we are offended. If our brother accepts what we say, we can reconcile the matter with our brother. If our brother won't hear us, we are to take someone to witness our efforts to reconcile the matter. If he still won't hear, we are to go to the Church. The Bible also tells us that we should go to our brother if we think he has an offense toward us, and we are told to take care of all offenses before we worship God. We are told to leave our gift at the altar, and reconcile with our brother (see Matthew 5:23-24). Biblically, our brother is the same as our neighbor and this can be anyone.

Forgiving an offense requires a desire to forgive from our heart. When we have the desire to forgive, the supernatural power of God will take over when our human ability has reached its limit. If we don't do away with offense, it becomes an open door into our mind. The enemy uses offense to introduce unclean thoughts that will eventually produce actions. Unforgiveness is the reason many people do not have the power to overcome sin in their lives. The enemy has an advantage over them because they are unwilling to forgive. Their violation of God's word renders them defenseless against the enemy, and gives him an advantage over them. Many people are not even aware that unforgiveness of God, others, or themselves is the reason why they struggle the way they do.

The Bible gives us an example of how bitterness can affect the human soul in Acts chapter eight. There was a man named Simon who was known as a sorcerer, and he had the people of Samaria deceived by his witchcraft. When the people heard Phillip preach, they received the gospel. Simon himself also became a believer and was baptized. He stayed with Phillip and witnessed many miracles. Peter and John came to the city when they heard that Samaria received the word of God.

When the apostles laid hands on the people, they received the Holy Ghost. When Simon saw them receive the Holy Ghost, he offered the apostles money to purchase the power of God. Peter told him his heart was not right, and to repent of this thought so he could be forgiven. He also made this statement. **"For I perceive thou art in the gall of bitterness, and in the bond of iniquity" (Acts 8:23).** The Jewish New Testament version of Acts 8:23 says, **"For I see that you are extremely bitter and completely under the control of sin!"** In spite of Simon's conversion, he was still controlled by sin because of bitterness. The word bitterness in the original Greek text means: poison, acridity. Gall has a similar meaning: poison or bile. Bitterness has a toxic effect on our body, soul, and spirit.

The Bible likens our spirit to a candle. "**The spirit of man is the candle of the Lord, searching all the inward parts of the**

belly" (Proverbs 20:27). In other words, our spirit is our conscience. The Holy Ghost will to lead the willing individual to righteous acts. When an individual has made up their mind that they won't forgive, they remain bound by their own will. The enemy then has free reign to operate through their soul. Jesus is more than able to deliver us, but He won't violate our will. We must be willing to forgive on a daily basis because there is a good chance we will be offended on a daily basis. When Peter asked Jesus how many times he should forgive, He said to him, "seventy times seven."

Then He spoke a parable about a man who owed money to the king. This man didn't have the money to pay his debt, and he and his family were to be sold to pay the debt. The man begged for mercy. The king was moved with compassion and forgave his debt. The same man went out on the street, and saw his neighbor who owed him money. The man's neighbor owed him less than the amount he had been previously forgiven. Yet, he had his neighbor cast into prison. When his neighbors saw what he had done, they were sorry and told the king. The king said to him, **"Shouldest not thou also have had compassion on thy fellow servant, even as I had pity on thee? And his Lord was wroth, and delivered him to the tormentors till he should pay all that that was due unto him. So likewise shall my heavenly Father do also unto you, if ye from your hearts forgive not every one his brother their trespasses" (Matthew 18:33-35).**

Jesus said if we don't forgive our brother we can't receive forgiveness or salvation. We can't be delivered from the sin that has us bound. The end result of unforgiveness is that we are turned over to the tormentor of our soul. The above parable reminds us that we have been forgiven a greater debt than anyone owes us. Keeping this fact in mind should enable us to be willing to forgive others. If our sins have been forgiven, we have become beneficiaries of the grace of God. The grace of God enables us to forgive and extend mercy towards others. Romans 12:8 lists mercy as a spiritual gift, and it is one that should be coveted by all. We should all have the desire to restore others as Christ has restored us.

Paul wrote, **"To whom ye forgive anything, I forgive also: for if I forgave anything, to whom I forgave it, for your sakes forgave I it in the person of Christ" (II Corinthians 2:10).** It takes supernatural power to forgive, receive the Holy Ghost, operate in any spiritual gift, and to be saved. We must repent of the sin of unforgiveness. Bitterness is a device used by the enemy to destroy society. Churches and families are under attack, and the end result is division.

If we are to overcome the enemy, we must be aware of his devices. Offense is one of his most subtle devices; he uses it to introduce his influence into our minds. Paul admonished us not to be ignorant of satan's devices. II Corinthians 2:11 says, **"Lest satan should get an advantage of us: for we are not ignorant of his devices."** Paul said he forgave every offense because he didn't want satan to have the advantage over anyone including himself. We mustn't allow the enemy to deceive us into holding on to offense. The forgiveness we have received from God should flow from us to others. When an offense is not dealt with, it becomes an avenue for deception. The end result is satan feeding his distorted thoughts into our mind. Many have fallen into sin, and have backslid because of offense.

The Bible is the final authority when it comes to salvation, and every other matter concerning God. The written word (logos) cannot be changed. There are many scriptures that tell us we must forgive everyone for every offense. If we seek God in prayer, He will speak to us through His spoken word (rehmah). He will be our counselor, and He will enable us to see others through His eyes. If we take into consideration that there are reasons why people act the way they do, we will look at them differently. God will enable us to love others unconditionally, and we will be able to forgive by the power of the Holy Ghost.

Forgiveness is one of the most powerful actions God enables mankind to perform. Forgiveness is more powerful than healing the sick or raising the dead. Although Jesus performed many miracles during His time on earth, there was none greater than the miracle of redemption and forgiveness He performed on the Cross. The Bible teaches us that only God can forgive sin, but He gives us the power to forgive as He does. In like manner God uses a willing vessel to heal the sick. Isaiah 43:25 says, **"I, even I, am he that blotteth out thy transgressions for mine own sake, and will not remember thy sins."**

In the book of Mark, we find Jesus healing a man of the palsy. Jesus said to the man, **"...Son, thy sins be forgiven thee" (Mark 2:5).** The scribes who were present reasoned in their hearts, "**Why doth this man thus speak blasphemies? who can forgive sins but God only?" (Mark 2:7).** Jesus knew what they were thinking. He said, "Whether is it easier to say to the sick of palsy, Thy sins be forgiven thee; or to say, Arise, and take up thy bed, and walk?" (Mark 2:9). The scribes were blind concerning Jesus' identity. When Jesus posed the above question to them, what He was saying was that forgiveness of sin, and healing both require divine assistance.

Jesus told His disciples that offense and betrayal would be among the signs of the end of the age. **"And then shall many be offended, and shall betray one another, and shall hate one another" (Matthew 24:10).** This sign is prevalent today, but Christians do not have to succumb to the sin of unforgiveness. We have been given the power to overcome sin and we must use it. We must be separate from the rest of the world. Jesus also said, **"And because iniquity shall abound, the love of many shall wax cold. But he that shall endure to the end, the same shall be saved" (Matthew 24:12-13).**

We are commanded to love one another. The Bible tells us that love abides forever. When all else fails, love will conquer. If we have God's love in us, and our heart is free of bitterness, we can endure to the end. Love and forgiveness will enable us to stand in the evil day. When we refuse to forgive, we give satan power. We are unable to defend ourselves against his influence because our will is in line with his. Again, harbored offense will render an individual powerless to overcome the adversary. Matthew 5:25 says, **"Agree with thine adversary quickly, whiles thou art in the way with him; lest at any time**

the adversary deliver thee to the judge, and the judge deliver thee to the officer, and thou be cast into prison." Jesus tells us to reconcile with our brother or we will be bound by the adversary. Forgiveness and love are requirements for fulfilling the greatest commandment ever given.

A scribe asked Jesus, What is the first commandment of all? **"And Jesus answered him, The first of all commandments is, Hear, O Israel; the Lord our God is one Lord: And thou shalt love the Lord thy God with all thy heart, and with all thy soul, and with all thy mind, and with all thy strength: this is the first commandment. And the second is like, namely this, Thou shalt love thy neighbor as thyself. There is none other commandment greater than these" (Mark 12:30-31).** Scripture teaches us that our most important relationships are in this order, with God, with others, and then with ourselves. Our relationship with ourself is important because it affects the other two relationships.

I have come to realize why Jesus said these are the most important commandments. If these commandments aren't being fulfilled, nothing else matters. Everything we can become in God, or do for God, depends on our ability to love as He does. It is not humanly possible to fulfill this commandment alone, but it can be done. Jesus doesn't ask us to do anything He doesn't enable us to do. We must take every offense to the cross, and nail it there in prayer. This includes offense against ourself.

As it has been stated in chapter three, shame is a grudge we hold against ourself. Shame is the root cause of self-destructive behavior. Deliverance from shame will only come to us when we choose to base what we believe in accordance to God's grace, and accept God's unconditional love. Grace is the unmerited favor of God. We must change our belief that God loves us according to what we have or haven't done. God loves us because of who we are. He doesn't love us less because of sin we have committed or more because of righteous acts. However, since God does not violate His word, our decisions can keep us from receiving God's grace.

Hebrews 12:15 tells us to look diligently less any fail the grace of God. Hebrews 12:16 says, **"Lest there be any fornicator, or profane person, as Esau, who for one morsel of meat sold his birthright."** Genesis 25:34 says that Esau despised his birthright. Jacob his brother deceived his father to get the birthright and the blessing (See Genesis 27:19-29). God was still able to use Jacob in spite of his dishonesty, but Esau did not believe in the promises of God. Therefore, Esau missed out on the blessing that God had for him. Malachi 1:2-3 says, **"I have loved you, saith the Lord. Yet ye say, Wherein hast thou loved us? Was not Esau Jacob's brother? Saith the Lord: Yet I loved Jacob, And I hated Esau, and laid his mountains and his heritage to waste for the dragons of the wilderness."** As long as we value our heritage in God, and see our worth through His love for us, God's love has the power to cover our sin.

As was mentioned in chapter three, we should be aware that a mentality of shame can be passed to us from our parents, and we can inherit our parent's way of thinking. In this case, shame is more difficult to overcome because we can't forgive ourselves for something we didn't do. However, we can overcome this mind-set or generational curse by the powerful blood of Jesus. Generational curses are belief systems that are passed down in families, and result in sin in the following generation (see Exodus 20:5; 34:7, Deuteronomy 5:9.)

The Bible also talks about those that have familiar spirits. These have to do with families as well (see Leviticus 19:31; Deuteronomy 18:11; I Samuel 28:8; II Kings 21:6; I Chronicles 10:13.) We must remember we are new creatures in Christ. We have a new lineage as sons of God. We must always bear in mind, we can be delivered when we make up our mind we want deliverance. We must choose not to let our past dictate our future. This is a battle, but not a losing one. God is on our side. Shame is not of God, but a result of the devil entangling his influence into our emotions. Our greatest weapon against shame is prayer, knowing the word of God, and putting that knowledge to use.

As stated previously, our most important relationship is our relationship with God. Secondly, our relationship with others. It is important to keep in mind that our relationship with ourselves will be a determining factor in our other relationships. This includes our husbands, wives, children, families, friends, and coworkers. When shame is present, all our relationships suffer. Consistent prayer is a weapon that will enable us to overcome shame in our lives because prayer increases our faith.

In the Hebrew language, prayer is defined by these three words: hymn, intercession, and supplication. The word hymn implies worship, to celebrate God in song. The word intercession implies praying for others. The word supplication implies making a personal request in prayer. These three aspects of prayer can be applied to assist us in fulfilling God's commandment concerning our three, basic, scriptural relationships (see Mark 12:30-31). When the basic principles of prayer are put into action, we will be ministering in love to each relationship. We are ministering in love towards God through worship, towards others through intercession, and towards ourselves through supplication.

In order to demonstrate the effect shame can have on our lives, I have included this information taken from Chester Wright's workbook, Conquering Shame. The cycle of shame is:

A: Shame Based Identity. I begin to associate myself with the person that rejection has convinced me I am, someone worthy of more and more rejection. I become convinced that I am hopelessly flawed as a person and that there is no power within me to change me (11).

When we see ourselves through the eyes of shame, we set ourselves up for failure. This mentality can result in behavior that will cause others to reject us. We are unable to move ahead because we keep repeating the same actions that result in more shame.

B: Distorted Thinking. I become convinced that I need someone or something more than I have within me to be happy, to feel complete, or to feel better about myself. If I could just find something more than I have within me to be happy, to feel complete, or to feel better about myself. If I could just find something outside me that is better than what I have in me, I could become a better person and feel better about myself (11).

Many times those with distorted thinking end up in marriages that lead to divorce because they are searching for someone to make them feel complete, but it is not humanly possible for their partner to fulfill this need. Also, distorted thinking leads to unhealthy sexual relationships that result in more shame for both individuals involved.

When someone's thinking has been distorted by shame, they are often preoccupied with their own needs. They are not considering the needs or feelings of another. Relationships where one or both partners think only of their own needs seldom succeed and usually produce more shame. On the other hand, shame can also lead to codependent relationships that are abusive in nature. The individual may rationalize their reasons for remaining in the relationship rather than making the decision to be alone. Also, the individual may feel that they are not worthy of any better treatment than that which they receive at the hands of their partner.

C: Acting out Feelings. I resort to searching for ways to fulfill my lust for things, pleasure, etc. This includes drugs, alcohol, adultery, perversion, gluttony, etc (11).

In this element of shame, an individual will attempt to fill the void that should be filled by God with the unhealthy things that the world has to offer. Many times these behaviors are rooted in self-hatred. Such things are destructive to the spiritual and physical man. They destroy an individual's health, can lead to problems with the law, financial ruin, and eventually death. These actions will leave an individual with more shame than they started with.

D: Life Damaging Consequences. The results of my actions obviously serve only to severely compound my problems. Now I must deal with the consequences of my actions, which have caused an intensification of my shame beyond my imagination (11).

To overcome shame and its effect on our lives, we must reach the place where we can allow God to love us. In order to receive His love, we must believe He loves us. When we are able to receive His love, we can love ourselves with His love. We must think of Calvary, and the proof of His love He gave us there. It may not be easy to forgive ourselves of our past sin and failures. Again, we can't do this on our own, but with God all things are possible. God's love covers a multitude of sin. We must remember that when we get to heaven these things won't matter. When our sins have been remitted in water baptism, they have been washed away. When we fall, if we repent, we have an advocate who is faithful and just to forgive us. We have to accept God's word by faith and hold on to it, no matter how we feel:

Shame has a distinctive life-style which is characterized by some specific attitudes which are especially damaging to ourselves and to our inter-personal relationships. Actually shame promotes a lifestyle of extremes in which we alternate between the extremes depending on whether we are "up" or "down." These extremes seem to be contradictory because they are so opposite in their character, but they are actually identical in their nature. They are simply two sides of the same coin. We manifest a particular extreme depending on whether we are "up" (attempting to hide our flaws, faults and shame in order to avoid rejection), or "down" (unsuccessful in our attempts to hide our shame, we surrender to it. We presume rejection and act in such a way as to produce it). (Wright 11-12)

I have included the above material because it was so beneficial to me, and I pray it will be to the reader as well. It helped me understand why I did the things I did, and why I remained in relationships with men that verbally and physically abused me. I understand why I felt the need to use drugs and alcohol. Even though there were times when I tried to involve myself in other things, the shame still existed. Eventually I would end up back in same place doing the same things.

I was never changed by doing the things that society calls acceptable; there was always something missing. The worst part was, I didn't even know what the problem was or why I felt the way I did. There are things I recall doing before I was delivered that appall me. I couldn't understand how I could have done those things. I understand now that the root cause of these actions was shame. Shame is a device satan uses to sink us deeper and deeper into sin. He is a predator looking for those who have been wounded by life's circumstances or their own mistakes. We can't afford to be ignorant of his devices to keep us bound. We must learn what his strategies are, and conquer them in our lives.

Shame is a stumbling block to the will of God in our lives. God never intended for His people to live in shame. Joel 2:25-26 tells us that it is God's will for His people to be restored, be given back what the years in bondage destroyed, to praise His name, and never be ashamed. Joel 2:27 says that He will be in the midst of His people and they will know Him as the Lord, and they will not live in shame. Joel 2:28 says, **"And it shall come to pass afterward, that I will pour out my spirit on all flesh; and your sons and your daughters shall prophesy, your old men shall dream dreams, your young men shall see visions."**

The children of Zion are also promised a great harvest. Joel 2:23 says, **"Be glad then, ye children of Zion, and rejoice in the Lord your God: for he hath given you the former rain moderately, and he will cause to come down for you the rain, the former rain, and the latter rain in the first month."** Zion is symbolic of the Church. The early and latter rain is symbolic of the outpouring of God's spirit in two different time periods. God has promised He will cause a spiritual rain to fall in the last days that will exceed the former rain. The former rain being the initial outpouring of God's spirit at the birth of the Church. James spoke again of the promise of the rain that would fall before the coming of the Lord. **"Be patient therefore, brethren, unto the coming of the Lord. Behold, the**

husbandman waiteth for the precious fruit of the earth, and hath long patience for it, until he receive the early and latter rain" (James 5:7).

According to Joel 2:23, the rain is coming in the first month during the time of planting. If we will plant the seed, God will send His spirit to make it grow. As the farmer waits for the spring and fall rain to produce his crops, so must we wait for the Holy Ghost outpouring that is to come. We are now living in the time of the latter rain, and God has only just begun to bring the harvest He intends. We must do our part to bring this harvest in, just as the farmer must do his part. We must remove every obstacle that causes us to stumble, and concentrate on doing the work that will bring in the harvest. We can do all things through Christ who strengthens us.

Paul warned that before the coming of the Lord there would be a falling away, and satan would again attempt to exalt himself in God's temple. (see II Thessalonians 2:3-4). The son of perdition has succeeded in deceiving some into following his doctrines instead of the written word of God. There was a great falling away during the time in Church history known as the dark ages. However, the hour has come when the truth of the gospel is being revealed, and light is being shed on the works of darkness. God is pouring out His spirit as He did in the beginning.

Those who stand fast, earnestly contending for the faith once handed to the saints, will be witnesses to the fulfillment of Joel 2:28. Shame can be a deterrent to the fulfillment of this prophecy, and to end-time revival. Shame is an enemy of unity and revival because our inability to love ourselves results in our inability to love others. Unity is necessary for personal and worldwide revival. God's people must be able to show His love to the world. This can only happen when we love ourselves.

When something goes wrong, our human nature has a tendency to blame God. God has never done any thing wrong, but we feel he is responsible for what happens to us. God has given man the power of choice, but not power over the consequences of his actions. Often the difficulties in our lives are a result of our own poor choices. Sickness and death entered the world when man chose to sin. Some people become angry with God because they have lost a loved one or because of a sickness. Bitterness or a grudge held towards God is rebellion.

Rebellion is what caused lucifer to be thrown out of heaven; he was the original rebel. He has been spreading his poison in the world ever since that day. Pride was involved as well, but his main transgression was that he rebelled against God's order. He wanted to be above God, to judge everything, and make his own laws. We have no right to be angry with God about anything. We must be grateful for His mercy. We have never seen the wrath of God. He has been patient with the world, in spite of its wickedness.

Rebellion is the root cause of problems with law enforcement, teachers, Pastors, and other authority figures in people's lives. It causes problems in every area of life. Rebellion is the reason many people can't get along with others at school or work, and some end up in trouble with the law. The

Bible says rebellion is as the sin of witchcraft. Those involved in witchcraft have made an alliance with satan. They are in opposition to every law of God. Jesus gave us the perfect example of obedience when He chose to die for the sins of the world so we could be forgiven. Forgiving every trespass should be a small thing for us when we remember His sacrifice

The Apostle Paul understood the need to forgive God and others. **"And herein do I exercise myself, to have always a conscience void of offense toward God, and toward men" (Acts 24:16).** Paul's statement indicates that it took effort on his part to keep his conscience free of offence not only toward others, but toward God as well. The word exercise used in the previous scripture implies to strive towards. Having a conscience free of offense obviously requires daily effort. The Bible tells us that the early Church prayed without ceasing. Paul must have been in prayer everyday to ensure that he was free of offence. We must follow Paul's example if we are to be free. When we don't keep our mind clear of offense, the offense will become bitterness.

The Bible tells us to get rid of bitterness, and lists the sinful actions that accompany it. We are exhorted to **"Let all bitterness, and wrath, and anger, and clamour, and evil speaking, be put away from you, with all malice: And be ye kind to one another, tenderhearted, forgiving one another, even as God for Christ's sake hath forgiven you" (Ephesians 4:31-32).** Every offense must be dealt with, but some are more difficult to forgive, and will require more time in prayer. When we have truly forgiven, the incident won't be remembered with hurt or anger. Our speech can indicate the presence of bitterness in our heart. It is written, **"out of the abundance of the heart the mouth speaketh" (Matthew 12:34).** In order to be rid of bitterness, we must will forgiveness from our heart. This means our desire to forgive is greater than the offence.

I heard a report from a Church in Mexico that I will never forget. The Church was having revival, and during service one Sunday a demon possessed man came in. He spoke in a guttural voice saying, "why are you taking Mexico from me? Why are you teaching these people to forgive? Forgiveness puts me out". In order to throw satan out of our lives we must forgive every offence. There are incidents that will trigger our memories to past offense, and many times satan will attempt to use the past against us. However, God may bring past incidents to our mind so we can forgive, and be delivered from the damaging effects of bitterness.

It is the will of God for us to forgive our brother for every offense. We are told to love and forgive each other. It is possible for us to live in peace with all men, as the Bible instructs us to in Romans 12:18. It is true that we all come from different cultures and different walks of life. We have all had different life experiences. We all have different gifts and calls placed upon our lives. God has created us all for a specific purpose to accomplish something special in His Kingdom. These things combined can create differences that affect how we relate to one another. For these and other reasons there may be conflict at times. Although it is not necessary to spend large amounts of time around all people, we are instructed to live in peace with all men. We must act like Christians in the presence of all people because we are written epistles to be read of all men.

We must always attempt to look at others through God's eyes. Knowing that God loves them, created them for a purpose, and died for them. We can compare people, with all their differences, to a painting with many colors. If we stand too close, the colors don't blend together properly, and there appears to be conflict. If we stand back, and look from a distance, the different colors blend to form a beautiful painting. The same is true of God's Church. If we don't agree with someone, we can love them from a distance. We can appreciate them for who they are in Christ, and what He will do through them for His kingdom.

Paul warns the Church that bitterness can cause trouble for everyone. It opens the door for iniquity, and causes us to lose the benefits of God's grace. **"Looking diligently lest any man fail the grace of God; lest any root of bitterness springing up trouble you, and thereby many be defiled" (Hebrews 12:15).** Paul admonishes the Church to be on guard against bitterness. Bitterness causes spots and wrinkles in the Bride of Christ. Christians must follow the example of Christ by forgiving as He has forgiven, in order to be "Christ like."

A revelation of God's unconditional love is our greatest weapon against the effects of bitterness that rob us of righteousness, peace, joy, power, and even salvation. When we are continually troubled by thoughts of the past, we must choose to put these thoughts away from us, and choose to think of other things. Paul instructs us to think on these things. **"Finally, brethren, whatsoever things are true, whatsoever things are honest, whatsoever things are just, whatsoever things are pure, whatsoever things are lovely, whatsoever things are of good report; if there be any virtue, and if there be any praise, think on these things" (Philippians 4:8).** We can use this scripture to measure our thoughts.

Our adversary learns our weaknesses by watching what we say, and what we do. This is why it is a good idea to discuss some things alone with God in a secret place in prayer. Psalm 91:1 says we can abide in the secret place of the most high. This is a safe place where we can tell God our problems, and the enemy can't get ammunition to use against us. When we pray in the Holy Ghost, speaking in other tongues, the enemy can't understand us. Also, earnest time spent in prayer will enable us to see things differently.

When we are having difficulty letting go of something someone said or did, it helps to remember that we have all offended someone at one time or another. Romans 2:1 says, **"THEREFORE thou art inexcusable, O man, whosoever thou art that judgest: for wherein thou judgest another, thou condemnest thyself; for thou that judgest doest the same things."**

We have no right to pass judgement on others. When we judge others for their faults, we are condemning ourselves. Often, we will find that those who have faults similar to ours irritate us the most. Could it be that we haven't dealt with our own faults? This may be the reason for our lack of tolerance when we see similar faults in others. When we examine ourselves instead of others, we can work on correcting our own flaws with the help of the Lord. We can't control what others do, but we can control ourselves. It takes time to break old habits, and to change the way we think. Our body, soul, and spirit will be made whole when we make forgiveness a daily practice. We will have that perfect peace the Bible talks about.

I Thessalonians 5:23 says, **"And the very God of peace sanctify you wholly; and I pray God your whole spirit and soul and body be preserved blameless unto the coming our Lord Jesus Christ."** We can't live a sanctified life when we choose to hold vengeance. God can't bless us when we willfully violate His word. Unforgiveness robs us of peace and adversely affects our health. The medical field has found that many diseases are brought on by bitterness.

An article written by Lisa Collier Cool called "The Power of Forgiving" further emphasizes the damaging effects of bitterness to our overall well being. According to this article, in the May of 2004 issue of Reader's Digest, 40 researchers at an Atlanta conference reviewed their findings concerning studies probing into the healing power of forgiveness. One found that forgiveness reduced chronic back pain. Another found that forgiveness limited relapses among women with substance abuse problems. In another study, the nonprofit Campaign for Forgiveness Research used MRI scans to explore how empathy and reconciliation effect the brain's left middle temporal gyrus. It is suggested that the brain might have a mental forgiveness center to be tapped.

Fred Luskin, PhD, director of Stanford University's Forgiveness Project, and author of *Forgive for Good*, has found that letting go of a grudge can cut stress by up to 50 percent. He reports that volunteers in his studies have shown improvements in energy, mood, sleep quality and overall physical vitality. Luskin says that carrying around bitterness and anger can be very toxic:

This is because our bodies are wired to treat any tension-inducing event like a crisis. It doesn't matter if it is a fire or reliving an argument. During times of stress our bodies release the stress hormones adrenaline and cortisol. These hormones prompt our hearts to accelerate, our breath to quicken, and our minds to race. Sugar is released into the blood to rev up the muscles, and clotting factors surge into the blood. This is harmless if it is a brief scare on the highway, but bitterness and anger are like accidents that don't end. As time goes by the hormones meant to save us are turned into toxins.

Bruce McEwen, PhD, director of the neuroendocrinology lab at Rockefeller University in New York City, says that cortisol wears down the brain, and leads to cell atrophy and memory loss. Cortisol also raises blood pressure and blood sugar. This causes hardening of the arteries leading to heart disease. Forgiveness seems to stop the flow of these hormones.

The American Psychosomatic Society performed a study on 36 male veterans who had coronary artery disease. They were burdened by painful issues, some war related, some tied to marital problems, work conflicts, or childhood traumas. Half of these men received forgiveness training; the rest didn't. Those who received training showed a greater flow of blood to the heart.

In a similar study performed at Hope College in Holland Michigan by psychologist Charlotte vanOyen Witvliet, PhD, 71 college students were hooked to sensors. They were told to relive incidents in which they were lied to, insulted or betrayed. When told to imagine forgiving the offenders, they experienced heart rates and blood pressure two-and-a-half times lower than when they thought about holding a grudge. Witvliet states that forgiveness could be a powerful antidote to anger, which is strongly associated with elevated blood pressure, and increased risk for heart disease.

In the same article by Collier Cool, Betty Ferguson tells her own story about the healing power of forgiveness. It is called "Forgiving the Unforgivable". In 1975, her sixteen-year-old daughter was murdered. She was so despondent she drank herself to sleep every night. This caused her to neglect her other four children. Day after day, she cursed the killer: Ray Payne, Debbie's English teacher, who abducted the teen before taking her life. Payne's conviction and life sentence didn't ease Betty's pain. "I was consumed by hatred," she says. And she suffered constantly with everything from headaches to back pain so harsh she could barely stand. In 1981, at her sister's funeral, a line from the Lord's Prayer struck her: "Forgive those who trespass against us." She began to read books about forgiveness---and began to feel it might be the answer. She visited Debbie's grave; the tombstone read "What the world needs now is love, sweet love." The refrain echoed in her head. Soon Ferguson was repeating the words "I am willing to forgive Ray" aloud like a mantra.

Within months, she wrote him. She told him she was done being mad at him. In 1986, eleven years after the murder, Betty visited Ray Payne in prison. She told him how much Debbie had meant to her, and how badly her heart had been broken. She said, "he listened, and we both cried." She left the prison a different person. She said, her heart felt "soft and light and warm." For friends appalled by what she had done, she had a ready answer. "Forgiveness is the greatest gift I ever gave myself---and my children," says Ferguson, who now works as a mediator in a Pennsylvania program for violent-crime victims. She says that forgiveness has not only healed her, it saved her life (Collier Cool 91-93).

Forgiveness will not only save our lives, but it will save our souls. Jesus is our example when it comes to forgiveness because no one has forgiven more than Him. Most importantly, we don't have to carry our burdens alone. Many suffer from mental stress that is caused by an unwillingness to submit everything, including offense, to God. Since Unforgiveness prevents prayers from being answered, including the prayer of repentance, refusing to forgive can send us to hell. Offence becomes a stumbling block that prevents us from moving forward in our walk with God. Psalm 119:165 says, **"Great peace have they which love thy law: and nothing shall offend them."** The word offend translated to Hebrew means: stumbling block or obstacle. When we allow an offense to get in our way, we will fall. If a soldier stumbles and falls during battle, he can't fight. Again, offense is the reason why many can't win spiritual battles.

We must always remember satan is a liar. The Bible calls him the father of all lies. He will try to put thoughts in our minds that aren't true. One of his tactics is to convince us we haven't changed or can't forgive. He will try to tell us that living according to God's word is too hard. It does take discipline and effort to live a righteous life, and to change the way we think. We must remember that we will reap the benefits of eternal life in heaven, and abundant life on earth. Jesus tells us that He came so we could have abundant life. The word abundant implies that we will have an advantage, more, and life beyond measure. We all know that life isn't a bed of roses. However, we can make the choice to sow good seed to everlasting life or bad seed to eternal destruction.

Whatever I am going through, I know my life is better now that I live according to God's word. I remember my how my life was before I knew Him. Now when trouble comes my way, I have the advantage. I have battles, but I don't fight them alone. Nobody can honestly say that living for God is harder than living lost in sin. The enemy always wants us to focus on the negative. We are warned that satan is working his plan of deceit on the earth. The Bible says, **"For the mystery of iniquity doth**

already work: only he who now letteth will let, until he be taken out of the way" (II Thessalonians 2:7).

The Bible gives us strategies that enable us to overcome satan. We are instructed in II Corinthians 10: 4-5, to cast down all imaginations and bring our thoughts into obedience to the word (Jesus Christ). We can't have authority over satan until we have accomplished this. II Corinthians 10:6 says, **"And having in a readiness to revenge all disobedience, when your obedience is fulfilled."** If we are to overcome, we must bring our thoughts into obedience to the word. If our thoughts aren't obedient to the word, we can't take revenge on disobedience. In other words, we can't take authority over satan when he has authority in our mind. We must fight him with the power God has given us. Always remember that satan has no power of his own. Our adversary's main tactics are deception and intimidation. We have been given everything we need to overcome satan. We give him power when we choose to violate God's word or focus on thoughts that are sinful.

Knowledge gives us power. The Bible says that God's people are destroyed for lack of knowledge. When we understand the root cause of our problems, we can work towards solving the problem permanently. For years I didn't know that my depression was related to unforgiveness. I received this revelation after I made a conscience effort to forgive. Now when an offense comes my way, I submit it to God in prayer immediately. I have learned that depression will follow an offense if I don't deal with it.

II Corinthians 11:29 says, **"Who is weak, and I am not weak? who is offended, and I burn not?"** Paul made it clear we all get offended. So don't be surprised when an offence comes. Paul told of the things that offended and weakened him, and the way he was treated by his own people. "**Of the Jews five times I received forty strips save one. Thrice I was beaten with rods, once I was stoned, thrice I suffered shipwreck, a night and a day I have been in the deep" (II Corinthians 11: 24-25).** Paul endured many trials for the sake of the gospel. Including mistreatment by false brethren, but Paul persevered through all these trials with the help of the Lord Jesus. And so can we.

Paul instructs us to put the past behind us, and to reach out toward our future in the Lord. "**Brethren, I count not myself to have apprehended: but this one thing I do, forgetting those things which are behind, and reaching forth unto those things which are before" (Philippians 3:13).** Paul was quite old when he was inspired to write this scripture. It doesn't matter how old you are. There is always more to reach for in God. So let's be strong in the Lord by the power of His word. Let's put on the full armor of God so we can stand, and not stumble in the evil days ahead (see Ephesians 6:10-18).

We can go forward, striving to apprehend a better life in Jesus Christ. I pray that we will give our vengeance to God. It isn't the will of God for us to hold on to it. God has great things for us to accomplish for His kingdom. We can't overcome the obstacles of everyday life, or the ones the enemy puts in our way, if we don't focus on what lies ahead. If we hold onto vengeance, we are holding on to something that doesn't belong to us. Let's give God our past and our vengeance, so He can give us a future.

Beauty for Ashes

My life was but ashes, I had only shame,

Constant disappointment, bitter disdain.

My plans came to nothing, to darkness I bade,

A path of destruction, mistakes I had made.

Days full of misery, nights full of pain

I knew no forgiveness, condemnation did reign,

One day at an altar, you became real.

A whole new outlook, suddenly I did feel.

You forgave all my sin, no questions were asked.

You gave all for nothing in spite of my past.

Victory for defeat, Joy for sorrow.

The knowledge that now I have somewhere to go.

If not for you where would I be?

You made a way, I finally see.

You gave beauty for ashes and that isn't all,

A new way of living, a brand-new call.

A life worth living, deliverance for all.

Chapter Five

Beauty for Ashes

What is God saying when He promises us beauty for ashes? I believe He is speaking to everyone on an individual basis. He is saying whatever you were before you knew me doesn't matter because I will make of you a new person. God is no respecter of persons. He will bring beauty into our lives regardless of our past. He will accomplish His good and perfect will in our lives, if we allow Him to. He will give us the power to become children of God, and rise above what we were in the past. We receive this power through faith and obedience to His word.

However, we are promised much more than eternal life. We are promised deliverance and peace in every situation, and we are given the ability to walk in newness of life. Every sin is washed away, and God keeps no record of our past sin. However, receiving beauty for ashes depends on our willingness give Jesus our ashes. Faith is required if we are to receive the beauty of entering His rest. Therefore, we must choose to believe. When we choose to exercise our faith, God will increase our faith. Jesus tells us in Matthew 25:29, **"For unto every one that hath shall be given, and he shall have abundance: but from him that hath not shall be taken away even that which he hath."** The children of Israel were promised a land flowing with milk and honey. It was the will of God to give them this land in exchange for the bondage of Egypt. Unfortunately, some of them did not have the faith to enter into the promise. We must be careful not to make the same mistake.

Paul warned us in Hebrews 4:1 to be fearful of missing out on the promise God has for us. Paul said we must put forth effort if we are to fully enter the rest that God has promised His people. Apparently, it is possible to fall short of receiving the full promise of God. In Hebrews 4:2 we are told that the same gospel was preached to all, but some lacked the faith to receive what they heard. Therefore, they did not benefit from God's promise. In Hebrews 4:3, Paul spoke of those who angered God with their unbelief. Whether or not God's people will enter His rest depends on their faith. Unbelief has been a stumbling block for many in spite of the fact that the promise was established in the beginning, even from the foundation of the world.

David spoke prophetically in Psalm 95:7-8; **"Today if ye will hear his voice, Harden not your heart."** Paul said David spoke of an appointed day yet to come because if Jesus had given them rest at that time, He wouldn't have spoken of another day. Paul made it clear that **"There remaineth therefore a rest to the people of God" (Hebrews 4:9).** Paul said that when we enter into God's rest, we cease from our own works as God did from His on the seventh day. When we cease from our own works, we are able to accept the grace God has for us by faith. We will no longer believe that what we did or didn't do makes us worthy or unworthy. We can believe in the unconditional love God has for us. Hebrews 4:11 says, **"Let us labour therefore to enter into that rest, lest any man fall after the same example of unbelief."** Paul admonished the Church to exercise their faith so they wouldn't fail to enter into God's rest as the children of Israel did. He made it clear that it will take effort on our part to enter into the full promise of God.

The rest we are promised is spiritual. Our Sabbath or rest is the baptism of the Holy Ghost. Isaiah 28:11-12 says, **"For with stammering lips and another tongue will he speak to this people. To whom he said, This is the rest wherewith ye may cause the weary to rest; and this is the refreshing: yet they would not hear."** Again, we must listen to what the spirit of God is saying, and labor to enter into His rest. We must choose to hear His voice, and not harden our hearts in unbelief. We must discipline our minds, and exercise our faith.

Jude 20 tells us that praying in the Holy Ghost will build up our faith. Praying in the spirit builds, and edifies the inner man. I Corinthians 14:4 says, **"He that speaketh in an unknown tongue edifieth himself."** The Bible says in I Corinthians 14:2, **"For he that speaketh in an unknown tongue speaketh not unto men, but unto God."** When we talk to God, He will talk to us. God wants to communicate with His creation, and restore the relationship that was damaged when man fell in the Garden of Eden. God is always reaching out to us, and speaking to us in so many ways.

I saw how God can bring beauty, and transformation into our lives through a common houseplant. I had an African violet that was almost dead due to lack of water. It looked as hopeless as I felt before Jesus changed my life. In a Pentecostal Church, I received the living water (the Holy Ghost), and was baptized in Jesus name. After this turning point in my life, I began watering the violet. I received newness of life by the power of God's spirit and His name. At the same time the plant came back to life. I continued to care for the violet, and it began to produce beautiful flowers.

As I cared for my spiritual man with prayer and fasting, the beauty of God's truth grew in my life. One day I noticed that something was eating the leaves of the violet, and cutting the stems off near the root. I discovered that it was an insect called a cutworm. I made up my mind that after that violet had come back to life, I wasn't going to let an enemy destroy it. I removed the worms, and used an insecticide to get rid of the enemy permanently.

Soon an enemy came into my life attempting to cut off my hope and faith, and to destroy everything that God was accomplishing in my life. I decided that I wasn't going to allow the enemy to come back to ruin my life. I used the word of God to fight the enemy, and continued on with prayer and fasting. I have gone on to tell others about Jesus, and what He can do for them. The violet has become a beautiful plant. It has produced fruit, (more violets), which I have given to others. This illustration shows us that when we control the enemy, instead of allowing the enemy to control us, there will be life, reproduction, and growth. We can cause growth in the kingdom of God by giving to others as Jesus has given to us. We can do as Jesus did, He went about doing good, and helping those who were oppressed by the devil.

For our protection it is important to stay in the will of God. Outside the boundaries of God's will are danger and deception. Deception will lead to our destruction. It is important to seek God's will for our lives. Prayer and fasting will help us determine the will of God for our life. We should also have all revelation confirmed by our Pastor. Any direction God gives us will always be in line with His word. Any other direction is not from God. We receive power and authority over the enemy when we stay under spiritual authority. The spiritual authority God has placed in our lives is our Pastor. Reading God's word and daily prayer will enable us to know God's will. We always want to stay in the will of God.

The following illustration is an example of what can happen when we are not where we should be according to God's will. One summer I planted tomato plants in my garden in the area I wanted them. As time went by, I noticed tomato plants coming up on their own where they had not been planted. I decided they must have come from the seeds of the previous year, and I let them grow. At the end of the growing season, I watched to see what they would produce. The tomatoes they produced were few, and weren't edible. The ones I had planted where I wanted them produced so much fruit I couldn't use it all myself. If we want to produce viable fruit in our lives, we must be willing to stay where God plants us.

Also, we must learn to trust God, and believe that He knows what's best for us. This isn't always easy. Especially when we are used to thinking we are in control. Again, we have to be willing to change our way of thinking. This is what Paul meant when he said we must labor to enter into His rest. We have to believe that God's plan wasn't designed to hurt us. Believing that God's will for our life is designed to prosper us is a sign that we believe God loves us, and it shows that we love Him.

Without faith, we can't receive beauty for our ashes, and we can't please God. Jesus tells us what we receive will be in accordance to our faith. We have great power available to us when we chose to have faith in God. The following scriptures demonstrate the power available to us when we choose to believe.

Jesus and His disciples were near Bethany when Jesus saw a fig tree. Jesus was hungry, so He went to look for figs, but He found none. The Bible says:

And Jesus answered and said unto it, No man eat fruit of thee hereafter for ever. And his disciples heard it. And in the morning, as they passed by, they saw the fig tree dried up from the roots. And Peter calling to remembrance saith unto him, Master, behold, the fig tree which thou cursedst is withered away. And Jesus answering saith unto them, Have faith in God. For verily I say unto you, That whosoever shall say unto this mountain, Be thou removed, and be thou cast into the sea; and shall not doubt in his heart, but shall believe that those things which he saith shall come to pass; he shall have whatsoever he saith (Mark 11:14, 20-23).

Peter, who is symbolic of the Church, commented on the condition of the fig tree. However, when Jesus answered, He spoke not only to Peter, He spoke to everyone. Jesus never overlooks anyone because He has a plan and purpose for everyone. It doesn't matter whether you have only recently heard the gospel, have been recently born again, or are renewing your relationship with God. You are a part of God's plan. Jesus tells us to have faith in God, and whatever we say and believe in our hearts will come to pass. We must ask ourselves this question.

Is what we say and believe based on faith or fear? Fear is the stumbling block that destroys faith. It is the opposite of faith, and was first seen in scripture when man fell, and sin entered the world. After Adam and Eve sinned they were afraid of God, and attempted to hide from Him. Sin and fear caused them to doubt God's love for them. The Bible tells us that faith worketh by love (see Galatians 5:6). The word worketh in the Greek language means energized. Faith gets its energy or power through love. We must be willing to take that first step, and open our hearts to God. This can be difficult when we have been hurt or rejected. It can be hard to trust when our trust has been broken. We must believe that God's love is not like the world's conditional love. God's love is unconditional. It is perfect love, and perfect love casts out fear.

Sin is what originally brought fear into our lives, and with sin came death. Jesus overcame sin and death, and the power it had over us. When we believe in God and His word, and we turn our backs on sin, we can overcome fear. Jesus tells us if we love Him, we will obey His commandments. When we make the choice to obey the laws of God, the Holy Ghost can do His perfect work in our lives. Grace then reigns through righteousness. Sin and fear will no longer reign in our lives.

When we choose to think and speak positively, believing the word of God more than the lies of the devil, our faith will grow. The Bible says every man is given a measure of faith. In order for our faith to grow, we must exercise it. The same is true of our physical body. If we want our muscles to grow, we must exercise them. Without exercise, our muscles will atrophy or grow smaller. Our faith is the same. When our faith is exercised, we can speak to the mountains in our lives and they will move. We can curse the things in our lives that keep us from bearing fruit. They will wither to the root and die like the fig tree Jesus cursed. Jesus can go back to where the problem began, and fix it forever. It will no longer bear evil fruit in our lives.

We can overcome our past when we believe in the power that God has given us. Jesus tells us in John 14:12, that if we believe in Him, we will do the things He did. We have been given treasure, and power in earthen vessels. No man who lights a candle will hide it under a bushel. Instead, he puts it on a stand for everyone to see. If we have received the baptism of the Holy Ghost, we should ask ourselves this question. Why did God invest His spirit in us? It wasn't so we could keep it to ourselves. God wants us to be light bearers in this world. Let's allow our light to shine before all men. Let's allow God, who is love, to shine in our lives.

Some people come to the Lord with baggage from past sin and failures. Some are backslid, and are bound by shame and condemnation. Whatever has happened in the past, we can't allow shame and condemnation to stop us from fulfilling the will of God. God will make a way for us, and He will give us beauty for ashes. He picks up the pieces, making a way for those seeking His will for their lives. The Bible says a just man falls seven times, and rises up again (see Proverbs 24:16).

We must rise above our past mistakes. Again, I use the example of King David. Many times he fell, but he always repented, and allowed God to pick him up. He continued to do great things for God because he believed in God's mercy and forgiveness. David loved God, and as a result, he trusted in God. Unfortunately, many people don't receive beauty for their ashes because they are unable to accept God's forgiveness. Sometimes we focus on our faults instead of the power that God has to change us.

We must fight every day to win the war for our soul by overcoming sin and our past. Remember that our soul and mind are synonymous. Again, the Greek definition for soul is heart, life, and mind. Our mind and soul is everything we are because it is eternal. The condition of our soul, and our decisions determine where we will spend eternity. How we think, and how we see ourselves, influences our actions and our walk with God. We must learn to see ourselves through the eyes of God. Thoughts of past incidents can come to us, and along with them come shame and condemnation. When this happens, we must remember what the word of God says.

The Bible says there is no condemnation to those who are in Christ Jesus (see Romans 8:1). Our thinking must be lined up with the word of God. When we repent, God forgives us. When we are baptized in the wonderful name of Jesus, our sins are gone. I was not raised in the Church. I did not hear about the Holy Ghost and baptism in Jesus name until I was 38 years old. I have a past that I am not proud of, but I know I have been forgiven because His word says so.

I want to take this opportunity to let the reader know that everything written in this book is intended to help others overcome. No statement is intended to be harsh or judgmental. The word of God judges, and that is what is presented here. I pray that everyone would have the opportunity to know the gospel of Jesus Christ, and have a personal relationship with Him. I am so thankful to be forgiven of my past. He has done so much for me, but I haven't forgotten who I used to be before I knew Him. I am learning everyday how important it is to give our past to God, and never take it back again. With the hope that it will help someone, I want to share something that I experienced.

Things were going great. I was thankful for my new life, and the privilege of serving God. At this time, I considered returning to college to be teacher certified. I received a call concerning my certification for substitute teaching. The call was in regards to a misdemeanor offense that occurred twenty-two years ago when I was a teenager. I was told that the state required a certified copy of conviction in order to determine if my certificate was valid, and I would be notified when a decision was made. After the call I became ashamed, afraid, and then depressed. Later that night we had our annual Christmas Banquet for the ladies of our Church.

Everything was wonderful. However, the call I received earlier in the day was affecting the way I felt about everything, including myself. I couldn't enjoy the banquet, and could hardly keep from crying. Looking back, I can't believe how one phone call affected the way I felt about myself, and life in general. This is why we can't base anything on how we feel. One problem was I was focusing on myself, and this is a very dangerous thing. When we focus on ourselves, we become a target for the enemy. Also, I was listening to the voice of shame. It was as if the incident had recently happened. When in reality it had happened over twenty years ago. We can't allow our minds to be controlled by shame. We must control the way we think, so we can control the way we act.

I spent time in prayer that night, and prayed the next morning. Finally, I called my Pastor, and he helped me put things in perspective. I thank God for his counsel. I realized then how easy it is for satan to build strongholds in our minds. I knew that if I allowed these thoughts to remain they would become a spiritual problem, and affect my life in a negative way. We must remember, **"Be sober, be vigilant; because your adversary the devil, as a roaring lion, walketh about, seeking whom he may devour:" (I Peter 5:8).**

We must always pray against deception. The devil is as a roaring lion, but he can't devour you with teeth because he doesn't have any. He takes circumstances or things people say, and twists them around to his perverted way of thinking. The devil looks for every weakness in our lives. We must identify our weakness, and build them up with the Lord's help.

There are times when God allows past incidents to be brought to mind because there are things from our past we have yet to overcome. However, God will never put more on us than we can bear (see I Corinthians 10:13). Little by little, He will heal us of our past. He can take the ashes of the past, and cause something beautiful to rise up out of them as a testimony to others. We must believe we are more than conquerors, and that the blood of Jesus has the power to cover past and present sin. Although we will reap what we sow, and many of our problems are due to our own poor decisions, God is merciful. He does not judge us according to our iniquities. He casts them into the sea of forgetfulness, and erases them from His memory.

While writing this book, I had the opportunity to teach Bible study to a woman with spiritual problems that were diagnosed as MPD (multiple personality disorder). She has a history of abuse, which seems to be a common factor in people who develop MPD. She also practiced burning candles to dead saints in an effort to invoke the power to foretell events, and have prayers answered. She told me her grandmother had the power to move things by looking at them. These things were passed down in her family.

This was acceptable to her because it was all she had ever known. She has a very large family. Many family members were involved in gang activity at one time or another. Because of the power of prayer, one of her sons brought his family to the Apostolic, Pentecostal Church that I attend. He began to tell the rest of his family about the saving gospel of Jesus Christ. It has been awesome to see God draw this extended family into His Church.

This lady has given me permission to tell what Jesus has done for her. All the glory belongs to Him for the wonderful things He has done, and for His delivering power. For many years this lady entertained these spirits. Since she was a child, they would keep her company when she was lonely. One manifested as her grandmother who raised her, and others manifested as children. They deceived her into believing they were her friends, and took advantage of her lonely childhood. When she would experience something traumatic, they would take over. Since they had control of her mind and emotions, she didn't have to deal with the trauma because she would "black out." When she was introduced to the truth of the gospel, these spirits began to manifest themselves aggressively, often expressing themselves in fits of anger.

She called the one of them "the beast." She said he was very large, and had thick black eyebrows. She said she would hear rumbling laughter when the manifestation occurred, and that she would feel like she was growing fangs and claws. During Church one Sunday, she was under the control of these spirits. I demanded to speak to her in Jesus name. The beast appeared in her countenance in an attempt to intimidate me. He left when I commanded him to go in the name of Jesus. He manifested on another occasion, and told me in a deep, guttural voice, "he won't go, she'll never be free." It doesn't matter what the devil says, when an individual wants deliverance, there isn't anything satan can do to stop it.

The word of God tells us that satan can't hold someone against their will when Jesus is present. The Bible says, **"And when he was come out of the ship, immediately there met him out of the tombs a man with an unclean spirit, Who had his dwelling among the tombs; and no man could bind him, no not with chains: Because that he had been often bound with fetters and chains, and the chains had been plucked asunder by him, and the fetters broken in pieces: neither could any man tame him. And always, night and day, he was in the mountains, and in the tombs, crying, and cutting himself with stones. But when he saw Jesus afar off, he ran and worshipped him" (Mark 5:2-6).**

A legion of demons couldn't keep this man from Jesus. When he saw Jesus, he went to him and worshipped Him. He must have made up his mind that he wanted deliverance, and that is what he received. The same is true today. Even when Jesus seems far from us, we must do as this man did. We must run to Jesus, and worship Him.

In spite of satan's attempts to keep her bound by MPD, when my friend chose to go to Jesus, she received deliverance. She received the Holy Ghost on a Sunday, and the following Wednesday she was baptized in Jesus name for the remission of sins. She was delivered, and satan had no more power over her will. The devil can't get through the blood of Jesus. We see a like figure of baptism in the Old Testament. The Bible tells us that after the Israelites went through the Red Sea; Pharaoh and his armies couldn't get to them. Pharaoh couldn't go through the Red Sea, and satan can't go through the waters of baptism.

It was my friend's decision to embrace God's commandment that delivered her from demon possession. God has made her a new person. It is written, all things are made new and old things are passed away. After her baptism, she said, "Since I went in the water, I don't feel the same." After we are born again, we are not the same. When we are baptized, we are buried with Christ. We are resurrected into newness of life through the Holy Ghost. The spirit of truth will lead us into all truth, if we allow Him. However, it is up to us to stay delivered. It takes effort on our part to change the way we think and act. We can't expect to stay delivered if we keep sinning or thinking sinful thoughts that will eventually produce actions.

The underlying cause of disorders involving the mind is sin. Again, I am not speaking of physical disorders of the brain, but of disorders that involve our thinking. Many times the root cause of these problems is unforgiveness coupled with a preoccupation with self. I make this statement in humility because it applies to myself as well as those who read it. Becoming aware of this fact has kept me delivered from the spiritual problems that used to control my mind.

We must take our eyes off ourselves, and put them on Jesus. It's not what we can or can't do, it is what He can do through us. It doesn't matter what anyone says, it doesn't even matter how we feel. Alone we are nothing, but the God within us is great and powerful. He will enable us to overcome any circumstance. As soon as we come to this realization, we will see things differently. We need the grace and power of God working in our lives. Jesus is the only answer to the sin problem.

He is the one with the power to remove the effects of sin from our soul. He will forgive us, and He will enable us to forgive others. He will help us manage any situation. Again, if we are to receive beauty for our ashes, we must be willing give Him the ashes. This can only be accomplished by trusting Him enough to let go. This is beautifully stated in the following poem by an unknown author.

As children bring their broken toys,
with tears for us to mend,
I brought my broken dreams to God,
because he is my friend.
But then instead of leaving Him
in peace to work alone,
I hung around and tried to help,
with ways that were my own.
At last, I snatched them back again
And cried, "How can you be so slow?"
"My child," He said, "What could I do?
You never did let go."

Finally, I must once more warn parents who have children with behavior problems. Don't give in to the system of this world where your child is concerned. Approximately fourteen years ago, a psychiatrist/counselor told me that if I didn't institutionalize my son for his behavior, he would end up in prison. I didn't know the ways of God, and I followed his advice. I allowed the system to handle my son instead of giving him love and discipline as the Bible teaches, and the system did not keep him out of prison.

In fact, I believe institutionalizing my son was the very act that mentally prepared him to go to prison. It made him feel angry and rejected, and gave him the frame of mind to accept those conditions. We cannot allow the system of this world to train our children. Putting my son in an institution to be drugged and counseled by the secular world never took care of his anger. Anger was the root of the problem. We must get to the root of the problem. The root cause of his behavior was never addressed, and my son ended up in prison by the time he was seventeen.

As has been stated, spiritual problems are often passed down in families from one generation to the next. I never knew my grandfather on my father's side of the family. I learned from my aunt that my grandfather was institutionalized in a mental institution for twelve years for a violent display of anger. She told me it took four police officers to hold him. This was many years ago when it was a common practice to put people in mental institutions for their behavior. Unfortunately, this sometimes happens today. When I heard about my grandfather, I was reminded of my son when I left him at Singer. He was only a child, but it took three men to hold him.

It has recently come to my knowledge that my grandfather's father died in a mental institution. He was placed there for similar reasons. Anger was passed to my father, and to myself, and then to my son, whose father has similar issues. Anger, fear, and depression all work together and are fueled by unforgiveness. In considering these things, I have come to realize how satan works in his attempt to destroy families. Our adversary will make every attempt to pass sin down to the next generation, and he will always kick us when we are down. Jesus will always be there to lift us, but He can't lift us if we don't reach out to Him. The blood of Jesus has the power to break these generational curses. There is no psychiatrist that can heal or deliver, and no magic pill. We need the delivering power of God.

Give your child to God, and not to this world. There are reasons behind behavior problems, and we need to look for answers. The answers won't come by drugging or institutionalizing our children. Many times we turn to the world's way because we don't know what to do; or don't have the time or patience to work with our children to find the answer.

Also, we are conditioned to believe doctors have all the answers, but they don't. Jesus is the only answer for the broken heart and wounded spirit. He has the answers we need in His word. He stands by watching and ready to help us. His word still works, it always has, and it always will.

Meanwhile parents continue to go to psychiatrists for their own problems, and their children's behavioral problems. The result is that doctors, psychiatrists, and drug companies get richer. This is sad because neither parents or their children receive any real help, and the root cause of the problem is never uncovered. The children never receive the guidance or discipline they need to send them in the right direction. Possibly all they need is to be loved and disciplined according to the word of God.

Many do not know there is a better way. I didn't, but I am thankful that now I can proclaim that there is. It starts with a willingness to believe, and obey the word of God. When we accept the promises of God by faith, we will receive beauty for ashes, and the Lord will be glorified. Many have been delivered by the power of God. They have given control of their hearts, lives, and minds to Jesus. By giving control to Him, we gain control of our mind through the mind of Christ.

WORKS CITED

American Psychiatric Association. ***Diagnostic and Statistical Manual of Mental Disorders, Fourth Edition, Text Revision***. Washington, DC, American Psychiatric Association, 2000.

Block, Mary Ann. Do, P. A. ***No More Ritalin: Treating ADHD Without Drugs.*** New York: Kensington Publishing Corporation, 1996.

Breggin, Peter R. M. D., and David Cohen, P.H.D., ***Your Drug May Be Your Problem: How and Why to Stop Taking Psychiatric Medications***. New York: Harper Collins Publishers, 1999.

Collier Cool, Lisa. "The Power of Forgiving: Best way to heal a heart." ***Reader's Digest***. May, 2004.

Easton, M. G. ***Illustrated Bible Dictionary, Third Edition***. Harper & Brothers, 1903

Rosemond, John. "How watching Television makes Kids dependent." ***Richmond Times-Dispatch*** 5 October, 2003.

Stern, David H. ***Jewish New Testament Commentary***. Maryland: Jewish New Testament Publications, Incorporation, 1989.